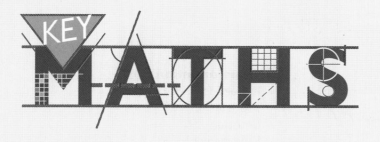

▶ **Roma Harvey**

▶ **Gill Hewlett**

▶ **Elaine Judd**

▶ **Jo Pavey**

T

Contents

Published in 1999 by:
Nelson Thornes Ltd

Reprinted in 2003 by:
Nelson Thornes Ltd
Delta Place
27 Bath Road
CHELTENHAM
GL53 7TH
United Kingdom

05 06 07 / 14 13 12 11 10 9 8 7 6

A catalogue record for this book is available from the British Library

ISBN 0 7487 4352 9

Illustrations by Oxford Designers and Illustrators, Peters and Zobransky and Clinton
Banbury
Page make-up by Tech Set Ltd.

Printed and bound by Scotprint, Haddington, East Lothian

Acknowledgements
The publishers thank the following for permission to reproduce copyright material:
British Broadcasting Corporation, p.44; Channel Four Television, p.44; ED 142018
The Thinker, Bronze by Rodin (front view) Musee Rodin, Paris/Bridgeman Art Library,
London, p. 173; Independent Television, p. 44; John Walmsley Photography, pp. 36,
59; National Savings, p. 135; Reproduced from the Ordnance Survey mapping with
permission of The Controller of Her Majesty's Stationary Office © Crown copyright
(07000U), pp. 189, 206; Sky Television, 44; Skyscan Balloon Photography, p.204
(bottom right); Sporting Pictures (UK) Ltd, p.209; ST(P) Archive, pp.125 (right), 227
(right), 230; The Hulton Deutsch Collection, pp.43, 63; The National Blood Service,
p.247; Tony Stone Images, pp. 11(John Lamb), 82 (John Lawrence);
www.johnbirdsall.co.uk, p. 130; York City Archives, p. 210.

All other photographs by Martin F Chillmaid.

The publishers have made every effort to contact copyright holders but apologise if
any have been overlooked.

1 Graphs

QUESTIONS

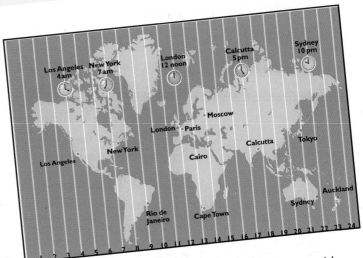

The map shows the time in different parts of the world when it is 12 noon in UK winter time.

Do you have any relations in New Zealand?
Be careful if you telephone them.
It is nearly 12 midnight in New Zealand when it is 12 noon in the UK!

Look in a world atlas to find out:

- how continents such as Africa arrange time zones to fit countries' borders
- what happens when a traveller crosses the International Date Line.

1 Plotting points

Tariq is using co-ordinates on his map to help him find his way to the campsite.

Axes	We draw a horizontal line and a vertical line known as **axes**.
x axis	The horizontal line is called the **x axis**.
y axis	The vertical line is called the **y axis**.
Co-ordinates	We use two numbers to mark a point. These numbers are called **co-ordinates**.

Point A has co-ordinates (3, 2).
We write this as A (3, 2).
This means point A is 3 **along** the **x axis** and 2 **up** the **y axis**.

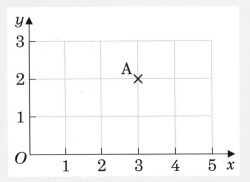

Exercise 1 : 1

1

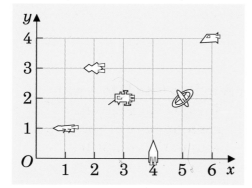

Write down the co-ordinates of each of these space vehicles.
The first one is done for you.

Buggy (2, 3)   Shuttle

Transporter   Cruiser

Star Base   Rocket

2

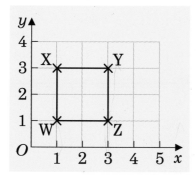

Write down the co-ordinates of these points.

a W

b X

c Y

d Z

3

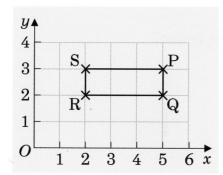

Write down the co-ordinates of these points.

a P

b Q

c R

d S

H1 **4** **a** On a grid plot these points.

      A(4, 3)
      B(4, 5)
      C(6, 5)
      D(6, 3)

    b Join the points in order A to B to C to D to A with straight lines.

    c What shape is this?

H1 **5** **a** On a new grid plot these points.

      L(1, 1)
      M(1, 3)
      N(3, 1)

    b Join the points in order L to M to N to L with straight lines.

    c What shape is this?

H1 **6** **a** On a new grid plot these points.

      E(1, 1)
      F(1, 5)
      G(3, 5)
      H(3, 1)

    b Join the points in order F to G to E to H with straight lines

    c What is special about these points?

2 Straight line graphs

Jeff plots 3 points on his grid   (2, 3), (4, 6) and (6, 9).

Jeff puts a ruler along his points. They are all in a straight line.

Jeff carefully draws the line with his ruler. He continues the line to the edges of the graph.

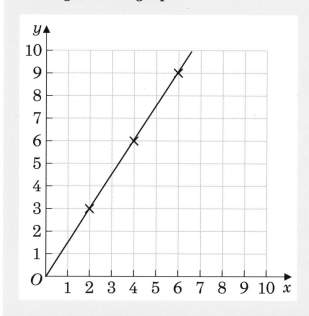

Exercise 1:2

 1 **a** Plot these 3 points on a grid   (2, 2), (6, 6) and (4, 4).

   b Use your ruler to check that all the points are on a straight line.

   c Carefully draw the line that joins the points.
   Continue the line to the edge of the graph.

 2 **a** Plot these three points on a grid   (3, 6), (5, 10) and (1, 2).

   b Check that all the points are on a straight line.

   c Draw the line that joins the points.
   Continue the line to the edge of the graph.

Jeff plots 4 points on his grid   (3, 6), (3, 1), (4, 8) and (2, 4).

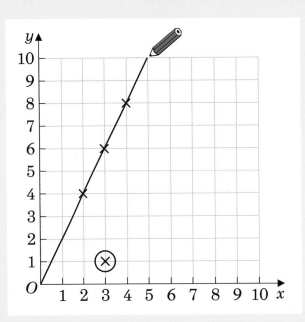

Jeff puts a ruler along his points.
One point is not on a straight line.

Jeff puts a circle around the point that is not on the line.

Jeff carefully draws the line through his 3 points with his ruler.

3 **a** Plot these 4 points on a grid   (1, 6), (3, 3), (2, 2) and (5, 5).

    b Use your ruler to check which three points are on a straight line.

    c Put a circle around the point that is **not** on the line.

    d Carefully draw the line that joins the points.

4 **a** Plot these 4 points on a grid   (9, 3), (2, 6), (3, 1) and (6, 2).

    b Use your ruler to check which three points are on a straight line.

    c Put a circle around the point that is **not** on the line.

    d Carefully draw the line that joins the points.

David is taking part in a sponsored walk.
He will get £1 for each mile he walks.

For   1 mile   he will get   £1
          2 miles   he will get   £2
          3 miles   he will get   £3

Exercise 1:3

 1 **1** **a** How much money will David get for 4 miles?

b How much money will David get for 7 miles?

David puts the information in a table.

Number of miles	1	2	3	4	5	6	7	8	9	10
Money in £	1	2	3							

c Fill in the gaps in the table.

David wants to draw a graph.

A **graph** is a picture. The picture shows how information is linked
to other information.

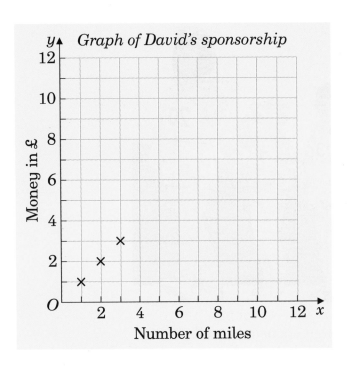

The x axis is miles.
The y axis is money.

For 1 mile he gets £1.
David plots (1, 1).

For 2 miles he gets £2.
David plots (2, 2).

For 3 miles he gets £3.
David plots (3, 3).

 1

2 **a** Plot all the points from your table on the graph on the
worksheet. The first three have been done for you.

b Join the points with a ruler.
You should have a straight line.
Continue the line to the edge of the grid.

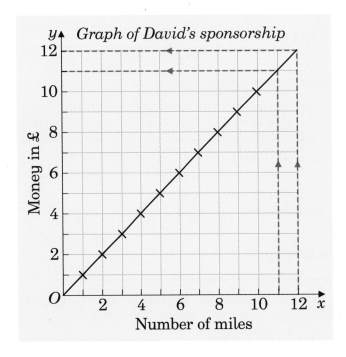

3 Follow the red line.
How much money
will David get if he
walks 12 miles?

4 Follow the green line.
How much money
will David get if he
walks 11 miles?

Sarah is taking part in
a sponsored swim.
She will get £5 for each
length she swims.

For 1 length   she will get   £5
     2 lengths she will get 2 × £5 =   £10
     3 lengths she will get 3 × £5 =   £15

Exercise 1:4

1 How much will Sarah get for 4 lengths?

W2 **2** On the worksheet fill in the gaps to work out how much
         Sarah will get for up to 6 lengths.

W2 **3** Put your information into the table.

W2 **4** Plot all the points from your table on the graph on the
         worksheet. The first three have been done for you.

W2 **5** Join the points with a ruler.
         You should have a straight line.
         Continue the line to the edge of the grid.

W2 **6** Use your graph to find how much money Sarah will get if
         she swims 10 lengths.
         Draw lines on your graph to help you.

7 How much money will Sarah get if she swims 8 lengths?
      Draw lines on your graph to help you.

Cooling water

You will need a cup of hot water, a thermometer, a clock or stop-watch, a ruler, and a piece of bendy wire or string.

Take the temperature of the water every minute and write it down in a table like this:

Time in mins	1	2	3	4	5	6	7	8	9	10
Temperature in °C										

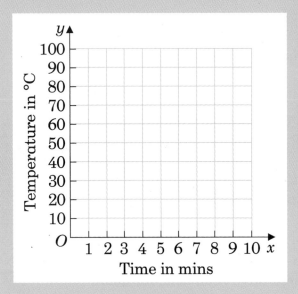

When you have all the readings, draw a graph.

Lay your ruler along the points to see if they make a straight line. They probably don't.

See if you can use a piece of bendy wire or string to make a smooth curve with your points.

If you find a smooth curve, draw it carefully without a ruler.

Graphs are not always straight lines.

3 Time

This is the most famous clock in the world. Most people think the clock is called Big Ben. Big Ben is the name of the bell.

The big hand on a clock tells the minutes.
The little hand on a clock tells the hours.

The time is four o'clock.

The big hand points straight up to the 12.
The little hand points to the 4.

Exercise 1:5

W 3   **1**   Write down the times on each of these clocks.

a 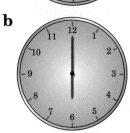   **c** 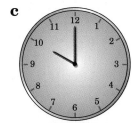   **e**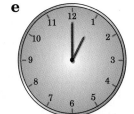

b 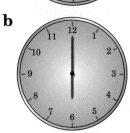   **d** 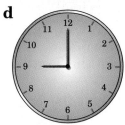   **f**

3 **2** Draw these times on the clocks.

    a Three o'clock   **c** Eight o'clock

    b Five o'clock   **d** Eleven o'clock

The time is half past eight.

The big hand points straight down to the 6.
The little hand is half way between the
8 and the 9.

 4 **3** Write down the times on each of these clocks.

a    **c**    **e**

b    **d** 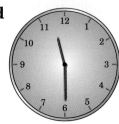   **f**

 4 **4** Draw these times on the clocks.

    a Half past one   **c** Half past seven

    b Half past four   **d** Half past twelve

The time is quarter **past** seven.

The big hand points to the 3.
The little hand is between the 7 and the 8,
but nearer to the 7.
It is quarter of the way **past** the 7.

W 5   **5** Write down the times on each of these clocks.

a 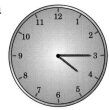   **c**    **e**

b    **d**    **f**

W 5   **6** Draw these times on the clocks.

    a Quarter past three   **c** Quarter past two

    b Quarter past eleven   **d** Quarter past five

The time is quarter **to** five.

The big hand points straight to the 9.
The little hand is between the 4 and the 5,
but nearer to the 5.

W 6   **7** Write down the times on each of these clocks.

a    **c**    **e**

b    **d**    **f**

6 **8** Draw these times on the clocks.

    a Quarter to six   **c** Quarter to two

    b Quarter to three   **d** Quarter to ten

Instead of using words to tell the time we can use numbers.
There are 60 minutes in an hour.
Start at 0 mins. Follow the arrow.

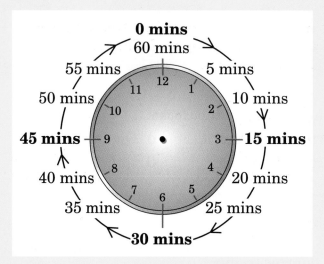

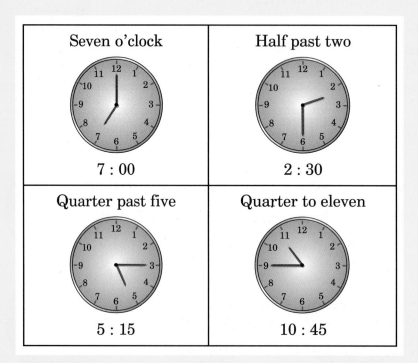

Exercise 1:6

 3, 4, 5, 6

1 Go back to Worksheets 3, 4, 5 and 6.
Fill in the empty boxes using numbers for the time.

 7

2 Write the time shown on each clock face in words **and** numbers.

Exercise 1:7

 8

1 Cut out the days of the week from the worksheet.
Put them in order starting with Sunday.
Stick them in your book.

 8

2 Cut out the months of the year from the Worksheet.
Put them in order starting with January.
Stick them in your book.
Next to each month write down a word, or draw a small picture, for something that reminds you of that month.

The calendar

| *Example* | It is Jason's birthday on 24th August. He wants to know which day of the week it will be. Jason's birthday is on a Wednesday. | **August** |

August						
S	M	T	W	T	F	S
...	1	2	3	4	5	6
7	8	9	10	11	12	13
14	15	16	17	18	19	20
21	22	23	(24)	25	26	27
28	29	30	31	...	...	...

Use Jason's calendar to answer these questions.

3 Write down the day of the week for each date.

   a 8th August   **c** 30th August

   b 13th August   **d** 14th August

4 **a** July comes before August.
     Write down the day of the week for 31st July.

   b September comes after August.
     Write down the day of the week for 1st September.

Not all months have the same number of days.

Here is an easy way to remember the number of days in a month.

Thirty days hath September,
April, June, and November;
All the rest have thirty-one,
Excepting February alone,
And that has twenty-eight days clear
And twenty-nine in each leap year.

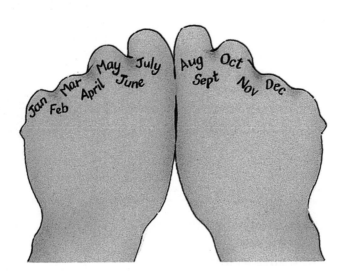

The months on the 'bumps' all have 31 days.
April, June, September and November have 30 days.
February has 28 days unless it is a leap year. In a leap year February has 29 days.
Leap years take place every four years, these are . . .
1996, 2000, 2004, 2008, 2012, . . .

5 Write down the number of days in:

   a January   **c** August

   b June   **d** November

6 There are 365 days in most years.
   How many days are there in a leap year?

4 Using time

Jeremy is ill.

He wakes up and looks at his clock.

It is eleven o'clock.

Jeremy doesn't know if it is eleven o'clock at night or eleven o'clock in the morning.

Next to his bed is an alarm clock.

The light is on next to **am**.

Times after midnight and in the morning are **am**.

Times in the afternoon and evening are **pm**.

Exercise 1:8

W9   **1**   Fill in the times on the alarm clocks.
Remember to colour in the **am** or **pm**.

W9   **2**   Fill in the times on the wall clocks.
Write **morning** or **evening** beside the clock.

Videos and timetables use the 24 hour clock.
24 hour clock times **always** have **four** numbers.

7.15 am	is written **07:15**
3 pm	is written **15:00**
Midnight	is written **00:00**
Mid-day	is written **12:00**

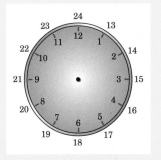

10   **3**   Fill in the table to show am and pm times in 24 hour clock time.

4   Write these times in 24 hour clock time.
(Remember we don't write am or pm in 24 hour clock time.)

a 2.15 pm   **c** 10.45 pm   **e** 5 am   **g** 11.30 pm

b 6.30 am   **d** 8.00 pm   **f** 3.15 pm   **h** 1.15 pm

5   Write these times in am or pm times.
(Remember none of the hours can be above 12.)

a 06:15   **c** 13:45   **e** 02:00   **g** 12:15

b 11:30   **d** 16:15   **f** 22:00   **h** 18:45

H 4   **6**   These things happened during Parvinda's day.
Copy it and fill it in.

	am/pm	What happened	24 hour clock time
a	7.15 am	Woke up	07:15
b	7.30 am	Got up	. . .
c	. . .	Had breakfast	07:45
d	. . .	Left for school	08:15
e	8.45 am	Arrived at school	. . .
f	. . .	Break	11:00
g	11.15 am	Break ended	. . .
h	12.30 pm	Lunch	. . .
j	. . .	Afternoon school	13:30
k	3.30 pm	School ended	. . .
l	. . .	Arrived home	15:45
m	5.45 pm	Had tea	. . .
n	. . .	Started homework	18::00
o	8.00 pm	Watched TV	. . .
p	. . .	Went to bed	21:30

G 4

1 Write down the co-ordinates of these points.

a A   **c** C   **e** E   **g** G

b B   **d** D   **f** F   **h** H

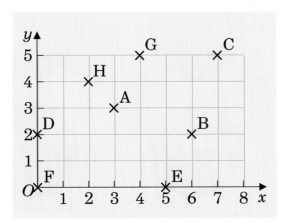

^H2   **2**   **a** Plot these 3 points on a grid   (4, 2), (6, 3) and (2, 1).

      b Use your ruler to check that all the points are on a straight line.

      c Carefully draw the line that joins the points.
Continue the line to the edge of the graph.

^W11   **3**   Gill is taking part in a sponsored swim.
She will get £2 for each length she swims.

      a How much will Gill get for 2 lengths?

      b How much will Gill get for 5 lengths?

      c On the worksheet fill in the gaps to work out how much Gill will get for up to 6 lengths.

      d Put your information into the table.

      e Plot all the points from your table on the graph on the worksheet.

      f Join the points with a ruler.
You should have a straight line.
Continue the line to the edge of the graph.

      g Use your graph to find how much money Gill will get if she swims 8 lengths.

      h How much money will Gill get if she swims 10 lengths?

4 Use words and numbers to write down the times on each of the clocks.

a

c
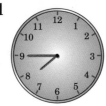

e

b

d

f

5 Here is a calendar for April.

April						
S	M	T	W	T	F	S
...	...	...	1	2	3	4
5	6	7	8	9	10	11
12	13	14	15	16	17	18
19	20	21	22	23	24	25
26	27	28	29	30	...	...

a How many days are there in April?

b What day is 1st April?

c Sam's birthday is on 17th April.
What day of the week is Sam's birthday?

d Which month comes after April?

6 These times are am or pm times.
Write them in 24 hour clock times.

a 1 pm   c 4.30 pm   e 5.45 am

b 3 am   d 10.15 pm   f 2.45 pm

7 These times are in 24 hour clock time.
Write them using am or pm.

a 15:15   c 21:45   e 11:00

b 06:30   d 23:15   f 12:15

2 Estimating your mental power

QUESTIONS

The number 10^{100} is called a googol.

This is a 1 and one hundred zeros.

10^{100} = 10 000 000 000 000 000 000 000 000 000 000
000 000 000 000 000 000 000 000 000 000 000 000
000 000 000 000 000 000 000 000 000 000

It takes Kerry $\frac{1}{4}$ second to write a zero and
$\frac{1}{5}$ second to write the 1.
How long does it take her to write a googol?

1   Squares and square roots

This number pattern is special.
The dots always make a **square**.

◄◄ REPLAY ► ►

one	**four**	**nine**
		• • •
	• •	• • •
•	• •	• • •
For 1×1 we write 1^2 (one squared)	For 2×2 we write 2^2 (two squared)	For 3×3 we write 3^2 (three squared)

Square numbers	The **square numbers** are **1, 4, 9,** ... We get them from 1^2, 2^2, 3^2, ...

Exercise 2 : 1

H 1

1   Copy this table of square numbers.
Fill it in.

1^2	2^2	3^2	4^2	5^2	
1	4	9			36

2 For 3×3 we write 3^2.
Write these in the same way.

a 4×4 **b** 6×6 **c** 7×7 **d** 9×9 **e** 11×11

3 For 5^2 we write 5×5.
Write these in the same way.

a 4^2 **b** 3^2 **c** 6^2 **d** 8^2 **e** 10^2

4 Use your calculator to work out:

a 6×6 **b** 8×8 **c** 9×9 **d** 12×12 **e** 14×14

5 Use your calculator to work out:

a 7^2 **b** 5^2 **c** 11^2 **d** 10^2 **e** 13^2

Does your calculator have a x^2 key?

You use the x^2 key on a calculator to work out square numbers quickly.

Example   Work out 6^2.

Key in: 6 x^2

Answer: 36

---

6 Use x^2 to work out:

a 3^2 **b** 4^2 **c** 7^2 **d** 9^2 **e** 12^2

7 Use x^2 to work out:

a 20^2 **b** 30^2 **c** 40^2

Trees

Trees have roots.

Numbers have square roots.

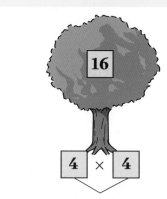

4 is the square root of 16 because $4 \times 4 = 16$.

These numbers are always the same for square roots.

Exercise 2:2

W 1

1 Fill in the missing numbers in the boxes.
The numbers for each root must be the same.

a

b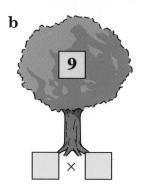

c

◄◄REPLAY►►

Inverse operations

Inverse means opposite.
Subtraction is the **inverse** of addition.
You can show the inverse by drawing
the function machine backwards.

Example

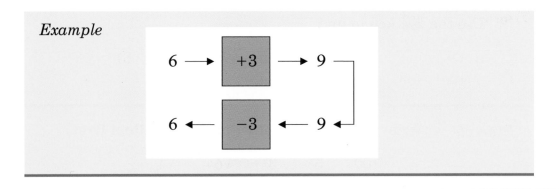

On a calculator there is a 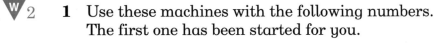 key.
This is called a **square root** key.

The symbol used for square root is $\sqrt{\ }$ or $\sqrt{\ }$.

The **inverse** of **square root** is **square**.

$\sqrt{\ }$ is the inverse of x^2

Example

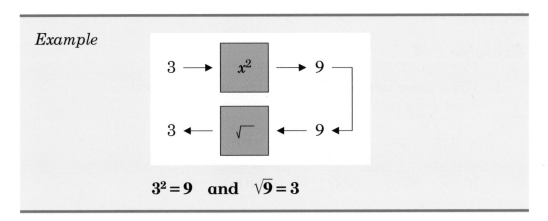

$$3^2 = 9 \quad \text{and} \quad \sqrt{9} = 3$$

Exercise 2:3

W2 **1** Use these machines with the following numbers.
The first one has been started for you.

a

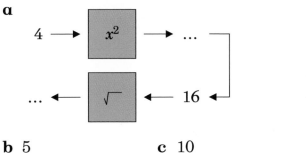

b 5   **c** 10   **d** 6

2 Use the $\sqrt{}$ key to find:

   a $\sqrt{9}$ **b** $\sqrt{36}$ **c** $\sqrt{49}$ **d** $\sqrt{81}$

Example   Write these terms in order of size, **smallest first**.

$$\sqrt{100} \quad 5^2 \quad 3^2 \quad \sqrt{64} \quad \sqrt{4}$$

First work out the answers for the terms.

$$\sqrt{100} = 10 \quad 5^2 = 25 \quad 3^2 = 9 \quad \sqrt{64} = 8 \quad \sqrt{4} = 2$$

Then write the terms in order of size starting with the smallest:

$$\sqrt{4} \quad \sqrt{64} \quad 3^2 \quad \sqrt{100} \quad 5^2$$

Exercise 2:4

1 Write these terms in order of size, **smallest first**.
First work out the answers for the terms.

   a $\sqrt{16}$ 5^2 $\sqrt{9}$ 6^2 $\sqrt{49}$

   b 4^2 $\sqrt{25}$ $\sqrt{36}$ 1^2 $\sqrt{81}$

   c 3^2 $\sqrt{100}$ $\sqrt{1}$ 6^2 4^2

2 Use your calculator to work out each term in order.
Turn your calculation upside down.
Write down the letters you see.
The answers to each line will make a word.

   a 2^2 $\sqrt{9}$ 1^2 $\sqrt{100}$

   b $\sqrt{1444}$ $\sqrt{5929}$ $\sqrt{25}$

   c $\sqrt{2025}$ $\sqrt{900}$

W3 **3** Draw a line to link the number key with its square.

4 has been linked to 16 because $4^2 = 16$

x	x^2
1	9
2	4
3	25
4	1
5	16

W3 **4** Draw a line to link the number key with its square root.

4 has been linked to 2 because $\sqrt{4} = 2$

x	$\sqrt{x}$
25	1
1	2
9	3
4	4
16	5

W3 **5** Draw a line to link the number key with its square root.

x	$\sqrt{x}$
9	1
100	3
36	10
1	7
49	6

2 Mental maths

Ruth, Andrew and Allison have £2 to spend on ice cream. They need to know which ice creams they can buy.

Sometimes we have to work things out in our heads.

Exercise 2:5

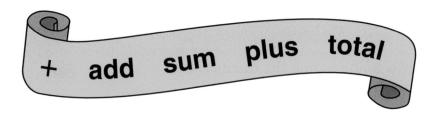

+ add sum plus total

1 Work these out in your head.
Write down the answers.

a 6 + 5	**b** 4 + 7	**c** 17 + 3
8 + 4	8 + 8	15 + 4
7 + 6	6 + 9	14 + 4
9 + 5	5 + 8	15 + 3
8 + 3	4 + 9	13 + 6
7 + 7	8 + 9	12 + 5

2 9 + 1 = 10   and   1 + 9 = 10
1 and 9 are a pair of numbers that add up to 10.

 1   Write down all the pairs of numbers that add up to 10.

Exercise 2:6

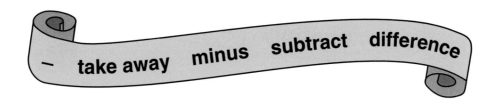

− take away minus subtract difference

1 Work these out in your head.
Write down the answers.

a $5-1$	**b** $10-7$	**c** $20-12$	**d** $15-12$
$6-3$	$10-4$	$20-15$	$13-11$
$4-2$	$10-3$	$20-17$	$17-14$
$7-6$	$10-9$	$20-18$	$14-13$
$8-2$	$10-5$	$20-13$	$15-11$
$7-3$	$10-2$	$20-16$	$16-13$

Example $7+9=16$

Using these numbers write down two subtraction sums.

$$16-9=7$$
and $16-7=9$

---

2 Use the following numbers to write down two subtraction sums.

a $8+5=13$	**b** $9+6=15$	**c** $5+9=14$
$...-8=5$	$...-9=6$	$...-5=9$
$...-5=8$	$...-6=9$	$...-9=5$

3 Write down two take away sums using the same numbers.

2, 3   **a** $7+6=13$ **b** $6+8=14$ **c** $7+5=12$

Multiplication

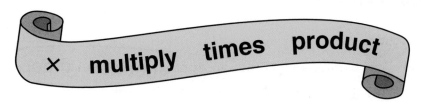

$\times$ multiply times product

Multiplication is a quick way to add lots of the same number.

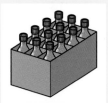

The quick way: 5 lots of 2
                   $5 \times 2 = 10$

Instead of counting the bottles in the crate
we say there are 3 rows of 4

$3 \times \qquad 4 = 12$

If $3 \times 4 = 12$, what is 4×3? $5 \times 6 = 30$, what is 6×5?
The answer is the same, 12   The answer is the same, 30

The order in which numbers are multiplied does not matter.

Exercise 2:7

 4

1 Copy and complete this
multiplication square.

Notice the **square numbers**
form a **diagonal** on the
number square.

×	1	2	3	4	5
1	1				
2		4			
3			9		
4				16	
5					25

2 Work these out in your head.

a 3×2 c 2×4 e 4×3

b 4×5 d 5×2 f 3×5

◀◀ REPLAY ▶ ▶

Multiples

If we multiply each counting number by 2 we get

1×2 2×2 3×2 4×2 5×2

or   2   4   6   8   10

Multiples   The **multiples** of 2 are   2, 4, 6, 8, 10, ... and so on.

Exercise 2:8

1   Copy and complete.

   a   The multiples of 3 start   3, 6, 9, 12, 15, ...

   b   The multiples of 4 start   4, 8, ... , ... , ... , ...

   c   The multiples of 10 start   10, ... , ... , ... , ...

All numbers are multiples of 1.

2   Multiples of 2 are even numbers.
Which of these numbers are multiples of 2?

    32   425   120   17   86   300

3   **a**   Copy and complete:
Multiples of 10 always end in ...

   b   Which of these numbers are multiples of 10?

    80   225   1000   110   40   305

4   **a**   Copy and complete:
The first four multiples of 5 are   5, ... , ... , ...
Multiples of 5 always end in ... or ...

   b   Which of these numbers are multiples of 5?

    35   87   170   58   600   115

W 5

5 Fill in the blank spaces on the multiplication square.

×	1	2	3	4	5	6	7	8	9	10	
1	1	2	3	4	5	6	7	8	9	10	Multiples of 1.
2	2	4	6	8		12	14	16	18	20	Multiples of 2.
3	3	6	9	12	15	18	21		27	30	Multiples of 3.
4	4	8		16	20	24	28	32	36	40	Multiples of 4.
5	5	10	15	20		30	35	40	45	50	Multiples of 5.
6	6	12	18	24	30	36	42	48	54		Multiples of 6.
7	7		21	28	35	42	49	56	63	70	Multiples of 7.
8	8	16	24	32		48	56	64	72	80	Multiples of 8.
9	9	18	27	36	45	54	63	72	81	90	Multiples of 9.
10	10	20		40	50	60	70	80	90		Multiples of 10.

6 Use your multiplication table to help you answer these.

a 6×5 **c** 7×8 **e** 6×7 **g** 8×9

b 7×4 **d** 9×10 **f** 9×5 **h** 7×7

◄◄**REPLAY**► ►

Factors

How many people can share 6 sweets equally?

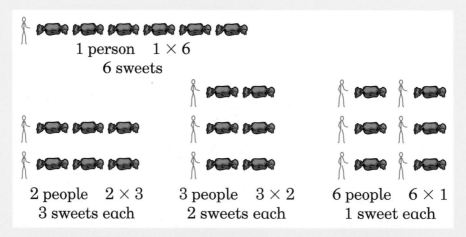

1 person 1×6
6 sweets

2 people 2×3
3 sweets each

3 people 3×2
2 sweets each

6 people 6×1
1 sweet each

The numbers 1, 2, 3 and 6 are the **factors** of 6.
They are the numbers that go into 6 exactly with no remainder.

Exercise 2:9

 4, 5

1 Find the factors of these numbers.
You can use counters or your multiplication square to help you.
The first one has been started for you.

a 8   The factors of 8 are   1, ... , ... , 8

b 12   **c** 15   **d** 16   **e** 20

Dividing

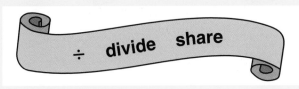

Dividing means sharing into equal amounts.

   Josh has a bar of chocolate
– there are 8 pieces.

If he shares them with Alan

 $8 \div 2 = 4$ pieces each

Josh   Alan

If he shares them with Alan, Barry and Carol

 $8 \div 4 = 2$ pieces each

Josh   Alan   Barry   Carol

If he shares them with Alan, Barry, Carol, Dave, Eve, Fay, Greg

Josh   Alan   Barry   Carol   Dave   Eve   Fay   Greg

$8 \div 8 = 1$ piece each

Luckily Josh does not have to share with so many friends.

Teachers have many different ways of writing division sums.

Exercise 2:10

1 Work out these division sums.

a $10 \div 2$ c $\dfrac{6}{3}$ e $9 \div 3$ g $6\overline{)12}$

b $5\overline{)10}$ d $12 \div 2$ f $\dfrac{14}{2}$ h $12 \div 4$

Example $4 \times 2 = 8$

We can write two divisions using the same numbers:
$8 \div 4 = 2$
$8 \div 2 = 4$

---

2 Copy these.
Fill in the missing numbers.

a $3 \times 4 = \ldots$
$\ldots \div 3 = 4$
$\ldots \div 4 = 3$

c $4 \times 5 = \ldots$
$\ldots \div 5 = 4$
$\ldots \div 4 = 5$

b $5 \times 3 = \ldots$
$\ldots \div 3 = 5$
$\ldots \div 5 = 3$

d $3 \times 6 = \ldots$
$\ldots \div 6 = 3$
$\ldots \div 3 = 6$

Example Use your multiplication square to answer this division sum:

$24 \div 6 =$

×	1	2	3	4	5	6	7	8	9	10
1	1	2	3	4	5	6	7	8	9	10
2	2	4	6	8	10	12	14	16	18	20
3	3	6	9	12	15	18	21	24	27	30
4	4	8	12	16	20	24	28	32	36	40
5	5	10	15	20	25	30	35	40	45	50
6	6	12	18	24	30	36	42	48	54	60
7	7	14	21	28	35	42	49	56	63	70
8	8	16	24	32	40	48	56	64	72	80
9	9	18	27	36	45	54	63	72	81	90
10	10	20	30	40	50	60	70	80	90	100

Answer: $24 \div 6 = 4$

H 3

3 Use your multiplication square to answer these questions.

a $30 \div 5$ **c** $2\overline{)18}$ **e** $\dfrac{48}{6}$ **g** $54 \div 6$

b $\dfrac{21}{3}$ **d** $35 \div 7$ **f** $\dfrac{36}{9}$ **h** $\dfrac{72}{8}$

3   Estimation

To estimate we often need to be able to round to the nearest whole number, 10 or 100.

On school sports day Linford ran 13.2 seconds in the 100 metres. His friend Colin ran 13.5 seconds.

Rounding to the nearest whole number

What is Linford's time to the nearest whole number?

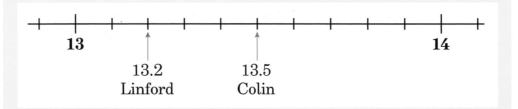

Linford's time is 13.2 seconds.
13.2 is nearer to 13 than to 14. It is rounded **down** to 13.
Linford's time is 13 seconds to the nearest whole number.
What is Colin's time to the nearest whole number?

Colin's time is 13.5 seconds.

13.5 is half way between 13 and 14. It is rounded **up** to 14.
Colin's time is 14 seconds to the nearest whole number.

If the number is half way between two numbers round up to the higher number.

Exercise 2:11

 1 Round the following times to the nearest whole number.

    a 18.9 seconds

    b 7.4 seconds

    c 23.8 seconds

    d 19.5 seconds

2 Tom ran 14.1 seconds. What is his time to the nearest whole number?

3 Linford also ran in the 200 metres race. He ran 29.8 seconds. What is his time to the nearest whole number?

4 Linford's tutor group's $4 \times 100\,\text{m}$ relay team came first. Their time was 49.2 seconds. What is this to the nearest whole number?

5 The table below gives some other results. Copy the table. Write the times to the nearest whole number.

Competitor	Event	Time (s)	Nearest whole number
Sean	400 metres	81.7	
Bill	200 metres	31.4	
Craig	100 metres	14.7	
Andrew	200 metres	36.5	

Rounding to the nearest 10

Severn Comprehensive School is
arranging a sponsored walk for
charity. The headteacher wants
a rough idea of the total amount
that will be collected. He asks each
group to give him their total to the
nearest £10.

Year 8 has collected £87 in sponsorship.
What is this rounded to the nearest £10?

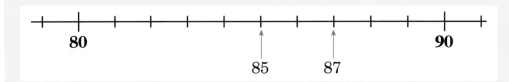

87 is nearer to 90 than to 80.
So £87 is rounded up to £90.

Year 9 has collected £85 in sponsorship.
What is this rounded to the nearest £10?

85 is half way between 80 and 90.
So £85 is rounded **up** to £90.

6 Listed below are the amounts of sponsorship collected by the
other year groups.
Round these amounts to the nearest £10.

    a Year 7 – £127   **c** Year 11 – £55   **e** Staff – £98

    b Year 10 – £74   **d** Parents – £106   **f** Governors – £62

7 Round these numbers to the nearest 10.

    a 16   **c** 48   **e** 256

    b 125   **d** 132   **f** 955

Rounding to the nearest 100

Examples   Round the costs to the nearest £100.

a

b

c

Tax and insurance £530   Tax and insurance £299   Tax and insurance £950

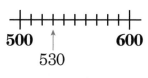

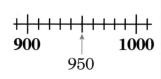

£530 = £500
(nearest £100)

£299 = £300
(nearest £100)

£950 = £1000
(**up** to nearest £100)

 8

8   Round these numbers to the nearest 100.

a 430   **c** 650   **e** 543   **g** 1950

b 790   **d** 320   **f** 787   **h** 842

Exercise 2 : 12 – a mixture

1   Round these lengths to the nearest whole centimetre.

a 4.6 cm   **d** 6.5 cm   **g** 9.9 cm

b 3.8 cm   **e** 8.1 cm   **h** 13.6 cm

c 5.9 cm   **f** 4.3 cm   **i** 13.5 cm

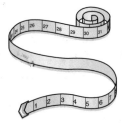

2   Round these numbers to the nearest 10.

a 18   **d** 55   **g** 99

b 46   **e** 91   **h** 48

c 57   **f** 52   **i** 101

3 Round these numbers to the nearest 100.

    a 127   **c** 757   **e** 411

    b 426   **d** 650   **f** 635

4 The length of a pencil is 17.2 centimetres.
How long is the pencil, rounded to the
nearest whole centimetre?

5 67 people took part in a sponsored walk.
How many people took part, rounded to the nearest 10?

6 A school raised £787 for charity.
How much did it raise to the nearest £100?

7 The Head of Highfields Lower School wants to know the
approximate number of pupils who have paid their
deposits for a school trip.

Here are the number of deposits paid from each year group.

    Year 7 – 37   Year 8 – 48   Year 9 – 52

    a Round the number of deposits to the nearest 10.

        Year 7   37 = ... (nearest 10)

        Year 8   48 = ... (nearest 10)

        Year 9   52 = ... (nearest 10)

    b The deposit paid by each pupil is £10.
Work out the deposits paid by each year group and the
total deposits paid.

        Year 7   paid $37 \times 10 = £$ ......

        Year 8   paid $48 \times 10 = £$ ......

        Year 9   paid   .... = £ ......

        Total deposits paid   = £ ......

    c Round the total deposits paid to the nearest £100.

1 $5 \times 5 = 5^2$. Write these in the same way.

    a $2 \times 2 =$ **b** $6 \times 6 =$ **c** $3 \times 3 =$

2   Use your calculator to work out:

    a 7×7 **b** 11×11 **c** 9^2 **d** 12^2

3   Write down the missing numbers from the boxes.
The numbers for each root must be the same.

a   **b**

4   Use your calculator to work out

    a $\sqrt{16}$ **b** $\sqrt{100}$ **c** $\sqrt{64}$

5   Write the terms below in order to size starting with the smallest first.
You will need to work out the numbers first.

    $\sqrt{9}$ 4^2 $\sqrt{25}$ 6^2

6   Work these out in your head.
Write down the answers.

    a $4 + 3$ **d** $6 - 2$ **g** 4×5

    b $7 + 8$ **e** $10 - 7$ **h** 3×5

    c $15 + 4$ **f** $20 - 14$ **i** 4×4

7   Write down the first 4 multiples of 3.

8 15, 8, 20, 12, 35

From the list above write down the multiples of 5.

9 The factors of 10 are   1, 2, 5, 10

Copy and complete:

a The factors of 6 are   …, …, …, …

b The factors of 12 are   …, …, …, …, …, …

10 Work out these division sums.

a $9 \div 3$ **b** $\dfrac{12}{4}$ **c** $5\overline{)20}$

11 Round the following numbers to the nearest whole number.

a 23.8   **b** 9.2   **c** 15.6   **d** 8.5

12 Round the following numbers to the nearest 10.

a 28   **b** 84   **c** 35   **d** 99

13 Round the following numbers to the nearest 100.

a 278   **b** 623   **c** 750   **d** 968

14 A man paid £756 for his car insurance.
How much did he pay

a to the nearest £10   **b** to the nearest £100?

3 Statistics: questions and answers

The first opinion poll was done
by **George Gallup** in **1935**.

Opinion polls are now often called Gallup polls.
Gallup is one of the biggest survey companies
in the world.

1 Diagrams and charts

◄◄REPLAY► ►

Pupils in class 8K were asked which was their favourite TV Channel.
Here are their results:

Favourite TV channel

Channel	BBC1	BBC2	ITV	C4	Sky	Other
Number of pupils	2	3	10	5	4	1

8K made a bar-chart of their data.
Here is their bar-chart.

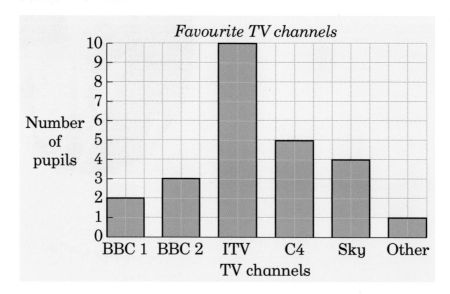

Look at the bar-chart.
From the bar-chart you can see:

4 pupils watched Sky.

The highest bar is for **ITV**.
ITV is the most popular channel.

We can check the number of pupils asked by adding
the numbers in each bar.
$2 + 3 + 10 + 5 + 4 + 1 = 25$ pupils

Exercise 3:1

1 Delroy asked the boys in his class which type of
TV programme they liked the best.
This is a bar-chart of his data:

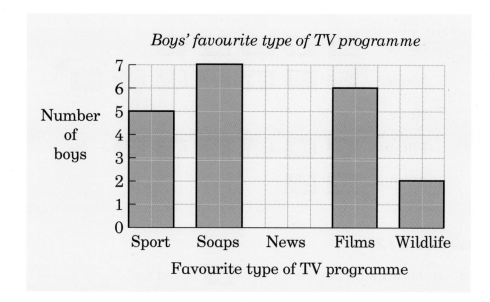

a How many boys chose films?

b Which type of programme was the most popular?

c Why is there no bar above News?

d How many boys did Delroy ask altogether?

W1   **2**   The pupils in class 8K wrote down the number of hours
they watched television on one day.

These are their answers.

Number of hours	None	One	Two	Three	Four	Five
Number of pupils	2	2	7	9	4	1

Draw a bar-chart to show these results.

Pictograms

Delroy now draws a pictogram to show his results
about boys' favourite TV programmes.
Delroy's pictures are all exactly the same.
They are placed in rows and columns.

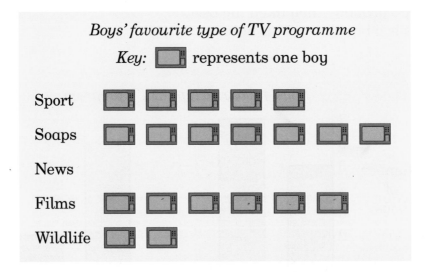

Exercise 3:2

1   a How many boys does one 📺 stand for?

b How many boys chose wildlife programmes?

c Using Delroy's pictogram, copy and complete this table:

Type of programme	Sport	Soaps	News	Films	Wildlife
Number of boys	5				

Next Delroy asks the girls in his class which TV programmes they like the best.
He now has results from all 30 pupils in his class.
It will take too long to draw 30 TVs.

Delroy decides to change his key.

Now ▭ will represent 2 pupils.

Key	A pictogram must always have a **key**. The key shows what each small picture represents.
Example	▭ represents 2 pupils ▯ represents 1 pupil
	▭ ▭ ▯ represents $2 + 2 + 1 = 5$ pupils

Here is Delroy's pictogram:

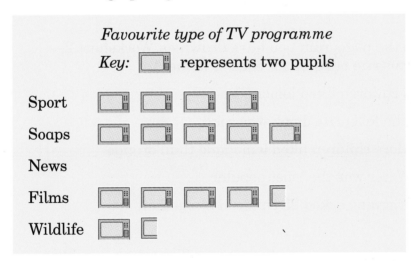

Favourite type of TV programme

Key: ▭ represents two pupils

Sport ▭ ▭ ▭ ▭

Soaps ▭ ▭ ▭ ▭ ▭

News

Films ▭ ▭ ▭ ▭ ▯

Wildlife ▭ ▯

2 **a** How many pupils chose sport?

 b How many pupils chose wildlife programmes?

 c How many more pupils chose sports than chose wildlife programmes?

 d Using Delroy's pictogram, copy and complete this table:

Type of programme	Sport	Soaps	News	Films	Wildlife
Number of pupils	8				

Lorraine asks her friends which drinks they like the best.

She grouped her results together.

orange orange orange orange orange orange
lemonade lemonade lemonade lemonade lemonade
coke coke coke coke coke coke coke coke
water water
apple apple apple

Lorraine puts the results in a table.

Favourite drinks

Orange	Lemonade	Coke	Water	Apple
6	5	8	2	3

W2 **3** Draw a pictogram to show Lorraine's results.

Use *Key:* ▯ represents 2 friends

W3 **4** Use the pictogram you have drawn on Worksheet 2.
Write **true** or **false** for each statement.

a 5 children liked lemonade.

b The favourite drink was coke.

c More children liked lemonade than orange.

d Water was the least popular.

e Lorraine asked 25 children altogether.

W4 **5** Five shops were asked how many T-shirts they sold on
1st May.

T-shirts sold on 1st May

Adams	Browns	Changs	Duval	Evans
16	12	10	20	6

Draw a pictogram to show these results.

Key: 👕 represents 4 T-shirts

Exercise 3:3

1 On 13th February Pat the postman delivered letters to 99 Hill Road.
The house was divided into flats.

The table shows the number of letters delivered.

Flat	99A	99B	99C	99D	99E
Number of letters	2	4	5	1	6

The bar-chart shows this information.
The number of letters goes up in twos.

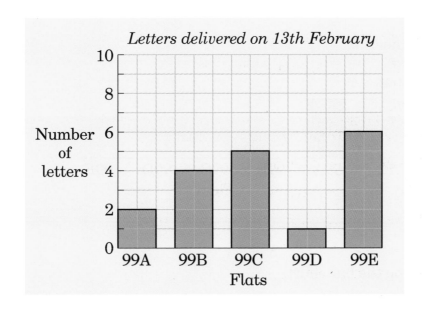

Use the bar-chart to answer these questions.

a How many letters did Pat deliver to Flat 99B?

b How many letters did Pat deliver to Flat 99D?

c At which flat did Pat deliver most letters? ·

d At which flat did Pat deliver least letters?

e How many letters did Pat deliver altogether?

H 1   **2**   Pat delivered letters on 14th February.
The table shows how many letters he delivered
to each flat.

Flat	99A	99B	99C	99D	99E
Number of letters	3	6	10	5	4

Pat has started to draw a bar-chart to show the number of
letters he delivered.

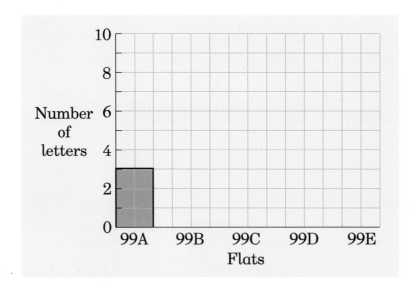

a Copy the bar-chart.

b Draw bars for the other flats.

c Give your bar-chart a title.

d Which flat got **most** letters?

e Which flat got **least** letters?

f How many letters did Pat deliver altogether
to the flats on 14th February?

g Why do you think he delivered more letters on
14th February?

Axes

The lines going across and up are called **axes**.
Axes must always be labelled clearly.

For example:

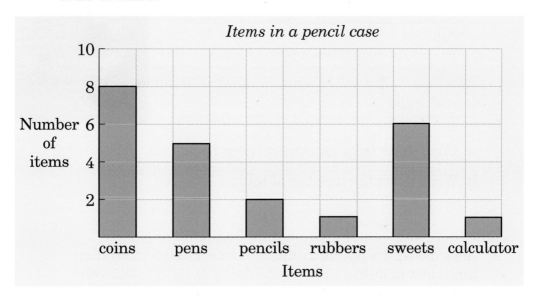

3   This bar-chart shows the number of items in the pencil
    cases of some pupils in class 8T.
    Use the bar-chart to decide if the statements below are
    true or **false**.

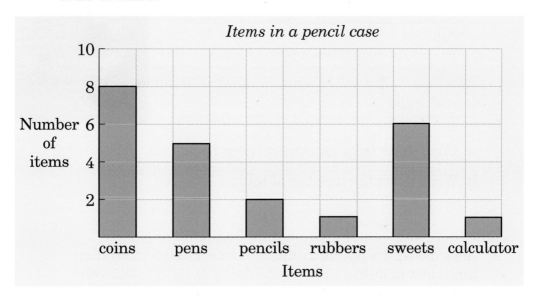

a There are more coins than sweets.

b There are more pencils than pens.

c There are 6 pens and pencils altogether.

d There are 4 more sweets than there are pencils.

e The number of coins and sweets added together totals 12.

f There are 23 items in the pencil case.

◄◄ REPLAY ► ►

Tally marks	Tally marks are drawn in groups of 5. The fifth tally mark goes across the other 4.

Example ||| This is three.   ‖‖ This is five.

JHT JHT || This is twelve.   JHT JHT JHT JHT This is twenty.

Exercise 3:4

1

Tally	Numbers
JHT |||	
JHT JHT JHT	

a Copy these tally marks into your book.

b Write down the number of tallies.

W 5   **2** Alice asked the pupils in class 8K how many videos they hired last month.

Here are their answers.

⓪ ⑥ ③ ④ ④ ③ ⑤ ⑦

⑤ ③ ① 7 0 5 8 6

Alice has started to draw a tally-table to show the number of videos.

She has circled each number when she has put it in the table.

Number of videos hired

Number of videos	Tally	Number of children
0	I	
1	I	
2		
3	III	
4	II	
5	II	
6	I	
7	I	
8		

Total number of children = _____

a Complete the tally column on Worksheet 5.
Circle each number as you put it in the table.

b Fill in the number of children column.

c Fill in the total number of children.

Data can be collected into groups.
You call this **grouped data**.

This can make diagrams easier to draw.

Alice puts her data into groups.

Number of videos	Number of children
0–2	3
3–5	8
6–8	5
Total	16

Alice then drew a bar-chart of her grouped data.
For grouped data the bars must touch.

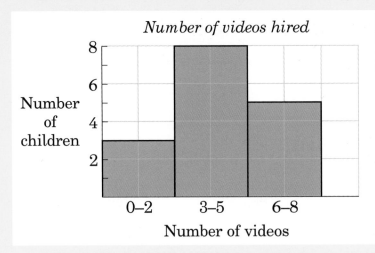

Alice then asked some of the pupils in class 8T how many
videos they hired last month.
Here are their answers.

Ⓞ ④ ⑤ ④ ⑦ ③ ② ④
① ④ 2 2 6 4 4 8

Alice decides to put her data into groups.
She has started to draw a tally-table.
She has circled each number when she has put it in the table.

Number of videos	Tally	Number of children
0–2	|||	
3–5	⑷H I	
6–8			

Total number of children = _____

a Complete the tally column on Worksheet 6.
   Circle each number as you put it in the table.

b Fill in the number of children column and the total.

c Draw a bar-chart of Alice's grouped data.

W 7   **4**   Simone's family had a party.
Simone wrote down the ages of everyone.
Here are the results:

(12) (59) (47) (52) (24) (43) (68) (38)
(49) (32) (69) (36) (45) (21) (29) (3)
47   42   55   18   54   41   53   34

Simone put the ages into groups.
She has started to draw a tally-table.

Age in years	Tally	Number of people
1–10		
11–20		
21–30	|||	
31–40	|||	
41–50	||||	
51–60	||	
61–70	||	

Total number of people = _____

a Complete the tally column on Worksheet 7.

b Complete the number of people column.

c Draw a bar-chart to show the people's ages.

d Give your bar-chart a title.

e Label the axes *Age in years* and *Number of people*.

f How many people were aged between 41 and 50?

g How many people were aged 20 or under?

h How many people were at the party altogether?

2 Pie charts

◄◄REPLAY► ►

Pie-chart   A **pie-chart** shows how something is divided up.

Example   8 pupils chose their favourite subject at school.
Here are their choices:

Maths, PE, French, English, PE, Maths, French, PE

First they must be grouped together.

Maths   Maths
PE   PE   PE
French   French
English

Then draw a pie-chart to show the favourite subjects.

2 pupils chose maths.
3 pupils chose PE.
2 pupils chose French.
1 pupil chose English.

Key: each slice represents 1 pupil

Keep the same subjects next to each other.

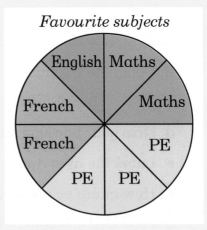

Favourite subjects

Exercise 3:5

 1 Brett asked 8 pupils for their
favourite colour.
They chose: red, blue, yellow, blue, blue,
red, red, red

Favourite colours

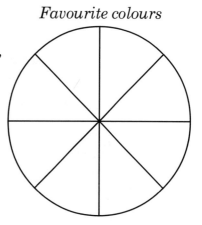

a Group the colours together.

b Copy the pie-chart.

c Colour it to show the replies.

d Write the name of each colour
on your pie-chart.

 2 10 people in class 8T were asked to name a capital city.

6 people chose London.
3 people chose Paris.
1 person chose Rome.

Capital cities

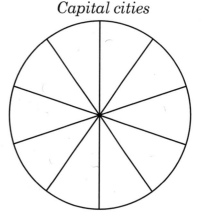

The pie-chart is divided into 10 slices,
one for each person.

a Colour in the pie-chart.
Use one colour for each city.

b Label the colours London,
Paris, and Rome.

3 Anna asked 20 people in her class
where they stayed on holiday last year.

Holiday homes

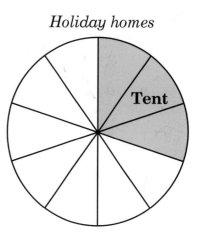

Here are Anna's results:
6 people said Tent.
2 people said Caravan.
8 people said Hotel.
4 people said Apartment.

Anna has started to draw a pie-chart.
Her pie-chart is divided into 10 slices.

One slice is used for 2 people.

Anna has coloured **3 slices** orange for the 6 people who stayed in a tent.

a Finish colouring Anna's pie-chart.

b Label the colours.

Exercise 3:6

1 Bill asked 8 of his friends for their favourite summer sport. The pie-chart shows his results.

One slice is used for 1 friend.

a How many of his friends said tennis?

b How many of his friends said swimming?

c Which sport did most of his friends say?

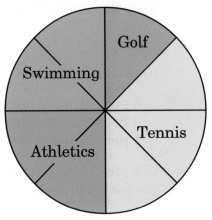

Favourite summer sport

2 16 children were asked which ice cream they liked best. The pie-chart shows their answers.

One slice represents 2 children.

8 children chose lollies.

a How many children chose cones?

b How many children chose choc ices

c Which was the most popular ice cream?

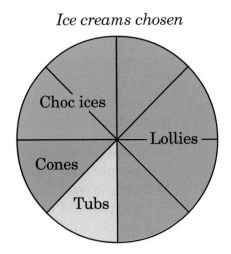

Ice creams chosen

 1, 2, 3

3 Collecting your own data

Exercise 3:7

1 Now you are going to collect your own data.

You will need a data collection sheet to record your results.

a Ask 10 children which of these items they have in their school bag.
Fill in the tally-table on your data collection sheet.

b Show this information as either a bar-chart or a pictogram.

c Did any of the answers surprise you?
Write down what you thought.

2 This time you can choose your own topic.
Keep it simple. Do not choose topics with lots of possible answers.
For example, you would be better to choose 'crisp flavours' or 'breakfast cereals' than 'favourite foods'.

Plan your work like this:
a Choose a topic.
b Name 4 different sorts.
c Write your tally-table.
d Ask 16 children which one they like best.
e Record your results.
f Draw a bar-chart or pictogram or pie-chart to show your results.

1 Janet the window cleaner came to Coronation Street.
The bar-chart shows the number of houses she visits each day.

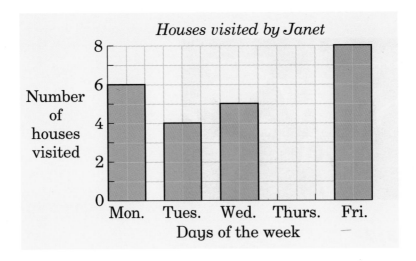

Houses visited by Janet

Number of houses visited

Days of the week

a How many houses did Janet visit on Friday?

b How many did she visit altogether on Tuesday and Wednesday?

c On which day do you think it rained?

2 30 pupils in class 8J were asked to name their favourite TV soap.
Their answers are shown in this table.

Soap	Westenders	Queen Street	Riverside	The Bikers	Here and Now
Number of pupils	6	3	9	8	4

Draw a pictogram to show the information.

Use *Key:*  represents 2 people.

W 12   **3**   Class 8F were asked which was their favourite school day.
The results were:

Friday	Monday	Friday	Tuesday	Tuesday
Monday	Tuesday	Monday	Tuesday	Wednesday
Friday	Tuesday	Friday	Tuesday	Wednesday
Friday	Monday	Friday	Tuesday	Friday

a Fill in the tally-table on Worksheet 12.
Circle each day as you put it in the table.

Favourite school day	Tally	Number of people
Monday		
Tuesday		
Wednesday		
Thursday		
Friday		

b Draw a bar-chart to show class 8F's favourite school days.

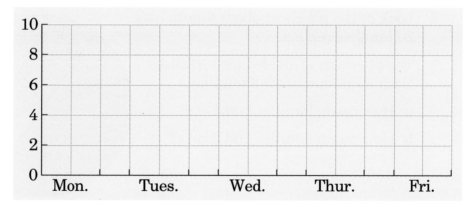

c Give your chart a title.

d Label the axes *Days of the week* and *Number of children.*

e How many children were asked?

f Which day did no-one choose as their favourite?

g Which day of the week do you like best?

4 Class 8J were asked how long it took them to get to school. The results are given to the nearest minute.

Time taken (minutes)	Number of pupils
1–5	6
6–10	3
11–15	5
16–20	4
21–25	8
26–30	4

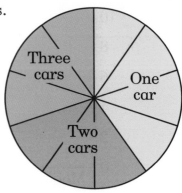

a Draw a bar-chart to show this information.

b How many pupils took 15 minutes or less to get to school?

c How many pupils took more than 20 minutes to get to school?

5 Look at the pie-chart about family cars. 20 families replied.

The pie-chart is divided into 10 slices. Each slice represents 2 families.

a How many families had 1 car?

b How many families had 2 cars?

W13   **6** 20 people were asked about their favourite drink. Here are their replies:

Tea	8	Coffee	6
Chocolate	4	Milk	2

Draw a pie-chart to show these results.
Use one slice for two people.

4 Algebra

QUESTIONS

**Muhammed ibn Musa al-Khwarizmi
c780–c850**

Al-Khwarizmi was a well known mathematician and astronomer who lived in Baghdad in the early 9th century. He wrote a book called *Kitab al-jabr wa al-nuqabalah*, which was about solving equations.

The word algebra comes from the word *al-jabr*.

1 Number patterns

Steve is making shapes with counters.
First he makes **L** shapes.

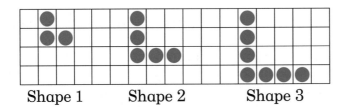

Shape 1   Shape 2   Shape 3

Steve has numbered each of his shapes.

Exercise 4:1

 1 **1 a** Copy the **L** shapes on to 1 cm squared paper.

   b Draw the next two **L** shapes and label them shape 4
      and shape 5.

   c Write down the number of counters used in each shape.

   d Now put your results in a table.

Shape number	1	2	3	4	5
Number of counters	3	5			

Copy and complete:

   e Each shape uses ...... more counters than the one before.

   f The rule is: add ...... extra counters each time.

Steve now uses his counters to make **X** shapes.

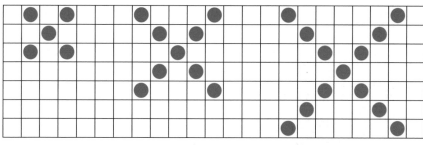

Shape 1   Shape 2   Shape 3

 2   **2 a** Copy the **X** shapes on to 1 cm squared paper.

b Draw the next two **X** shapes and label them shape 4 and shape 5.

c Write down the number of counters used in each shape.

d Now put your results in a table.

Shape number	1	2	3	4	5
Number of counters	5	9			

Copy and complete:

e Each shape uses ...... more counters than the one before.

f The rule is: add ...... extra counters each time.

Steve finally decides to make **Y** shapes

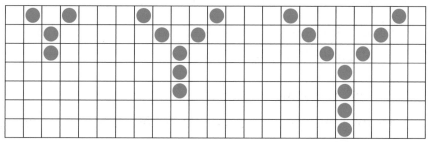

Shape 1   Shape 2   Shape 3

3

3 **a** Copy the Y shapes on to 1 cm squared paper.

b Draw the next two Y shapes and label them shape 4 and shape 5.

c Write down the number of counters used in each shape.

d Now put your results in a table.

Shape number	1	2	3	4	5
Number of counters	4	7			

Copy and complete:

e Each shape uses …… more counters than the one before.

f The rule is: add …… extra counters each time.

◄◄REPLAY►►

When you use a **rule** you get a **number pattern**.

The **even numbers** are an example of a number pattern.

2, 4, 6, 8, 10   The starting number is   2.
                    The rule is   *add 2 or +2 each time.*

The next two numbers in the pattern are 12 and 14.

Exercise 4:2

1 For each number pattern write down the **rule** and the next **two** numbers.

a 1, 3, 5, 7, 9   **d** 6, 9, 12, 15, 18

b 10, 20, 30, 40, 50   **e** 20, 40, 60, 80, 100

1, 2

c 15, 20, 25, 30, 35   **f** 12, 16, 20, 24, 28

Rules and robots

You can use robots to help you with number patterns.

3 —→ +6 —→ 9

This robot screen gives the rule.

The rule is *add 6*.

Exercise 4:3

1 Write down the answer for each robot.

a   2 —→ +5 —→ ?

c   7 —→ −2 —→ ?

b   6 —→ −3 —→ ?

d   4 —→ +3 —→ ?

Sometimes we need to work out what the screens should show.

Example

2 —→ ? —→ 8

The screen should show +6

2 Write down the rule that belongs on each robot screen.

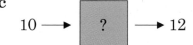

a   4 —→ ? —→ 9

c   10 —→ ? —→ 12

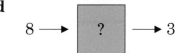

b   6 —→ ? —→ 5

d   8 —→ ? —→ 3

We can use **one** robot to give the **same** rule for more than one set of numbers.

Example

Find the **same** rule that fits **both** these screens.

 and

There are 2 rules that could fit the first robot screen.

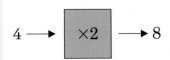

and

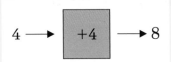

Only one of **these** rules fits the second robot screen.

6 ⟶ +4 ⟶ 10

The rule that fits both robot screens is +4

4 ⟶ +4 ⟶ 8
6 ⟶   ⟶ 10

Exercise 4:4

 1 Choose **one** rule that will fit both robot screens.

a Choose from:

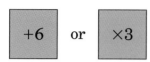

$$3 \longrightarrow \boxed{?} \longrightarrow 9$$

$$2 \longrightarrow \boxed{?} \longrightarrow 6$$

Answer:

b Choose from:

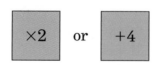

$$4 \longrightarrow \boxed{?} \longrightarrow 8$$

$$3 \longrightarrow \boxed{?} \longrightarrow 7$$

c Choose from:

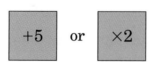

$$10 \longrightarrow \boxed{?} \longrightarrow 15$$

$$5 \longrightarrow \boxed{?} \longrightarrow 10$$

2 Find the rule that fits both robot screens.

a $7 \longrightarrow \boxed{?} \longrightarrow 14$

$9 \longrightarrow \boxed{?} \longrightarrow 18$

c $2 \longrightarrow \boxed{?} \longrightarrow 8$

$4 \longrightarrow \boxed{?} \longrightarrow 16$

b $4 \longrightarrow \boxed{?} \longrightarrow 12$

$2 \longrightarrow \boxed{?} \longrightarrow 10$

d $5 \longrightarrow \boxed{?} \longrightarrow 10$

$6 \longrightarrow \boxed{?} \longrightarrow 11$

2 Finding your own rules

....

Finding formulas

Lizzy is making triangles out of matchsticks.

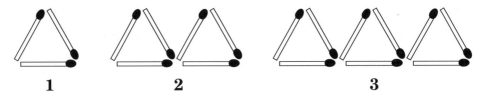

1   2   3

Lizzy counts the number of matches she uses in each diagram.

She puts her results in a table:

Number of triangles	1	2	3	4	5
Number of matchsticks	3	6	9	12	15

+3   +3   +3   +3

Lizzy uses 3 extra matchsticks each time so the **rule** is +3.

If Lizzy knows the number of triangles she wants to make, she can work out the number of matches she will need.

To do this she needs to find a **formula**.

She needs to find a robot which will fit any number of triangles.

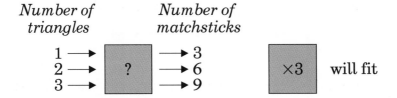

Number of triangles   *Number of matchsticks*

1 ⟶   ⟶ 3
2 ⟶   ?   ⟶ 6   ×3   will fit
3 ⟶   ⟶ 9

The formula can be written as:

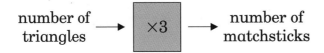

number of triangles ⟶ ×3 ⟶ number of matchsticks

or
number of matchsticks = 3 times the number of triangles

Exercise 4:5

1 Lizzy now makes squares out of matchsticks.

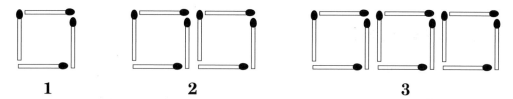

1   **2**   **3**

She counts the number of matchsticks she has used each time.

Her results are in the table:

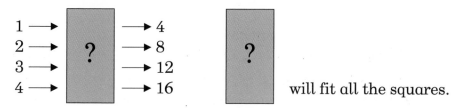

Number of squares	1	2	3	4
Number of matchsticks	4	8	12	16

+?   +?   +?

a How many extra matches has she used each time?

b Find the robot that will fit any number of squares.

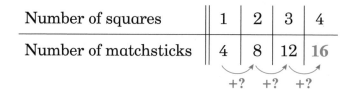

1 ⟶ ? ⟶ 4
2 ⟶ ? ⟶ 8
3 ⟶ ? ⟶ 12
4 ⟶ ? ⟶ 16

? will fit all the squares.

c Write the formula using a robot.

number of ... ⟶ ? ⟶ number of ...

Notice that in both cases the rule has helped us to decide what to multiply by for the formula.

Rule   +3
Formula ×3

Rule   +4
Formula ×4

1 **2** Using the results given in the tables write down the rule and the formula.

a

Number of diagram	1	2	3	4
Number of matchsticks	5	10	15	20

c

Number of diagram	1	2	3	4
Number of matchsticks	6	12	18	24

b

Number of diagram	1	2	3	4
Number of matchsticks	2	4	6	8

d

Number of diagram	1	2	3	4
Number of matchsticks	10	20	30	40

Example   The formula for the triangles is:

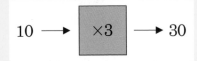

We can use this formula to work out the number of matchsticks in any number of triangles.

Use this formula to find the number of matchsticks in 10 triangles.

$$10 \longrightarrow \boxed{\times 3} \longrightarrow 30$$

Answer: 30 matchsticks.

---

3 Use the triangle formula to find the number of matchsticks in:

    a 6 triangles   **b** 20 triangles   **c** 100 triangles.

4 The formula for the number of matchsticks in pentagons is:

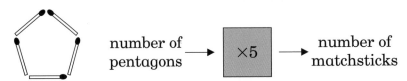

Use this formula to find the number of matchsticks in:

    a 6 pentagons   **b** 8 pentagons   **c** 10 pentagons.

Formulas can also be written in words or letters.

number of *t*riangles $\longrightarrow$ $\boxed{\times 3}$ $\longrightarrow$ number of *m*atchsticks

can be written as:

number of *m*atchsticks = 3 times the number of *t*riangles

or $\qquad m = 3 \times t$

H 2

5 Write the formulas given as robots in words and letters.

a

number of *s*quares $\longrightarrow$ $\boxed{\times 4}$ $\longrightarrow$ number of *m*atchsticks

Number of *m*atchsticks = ... times the number of *s*quares

$\qquad m = \ldots \times s$

b

number of *h*exagons $\longrightarrow$ $\boxed{\times 6}$ $\longrightarrow$ number of *m*atchsticks

Number of *m*atchsticks = ... times the number of *h*exagons

$\qquad m = \ldots \times h$

c

number of *p*entagons $\longrightarrow$ $\boxed{\times 5}$ $\longrightarrow$ number of *m*atchsticks

Number of .... = ... times the number of ....

$\qquad m = \ldots \times \ldots$

d

number of *o*ctagons $\longrightarrow$ $\boxed{\times 8}$ $\longrightarrow$ number of *m*atchsticks

Number of .... = ... times ....

$\qquad m = \ldots \times \ldots$

Example　The formula for the triangles is:

number of *m*atchsticks = **3** times the number of *t*riangles

Use the formula to find the number of matchsticks for **10** triangles.

Number of matchsticks $= 3 \times 10$
$$= 30$$

Exercise 4:6

1 Apples are sold in trays of 4.

Number of *a*pples = **4** times number of *t*rays

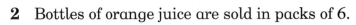

Use this formula to find the number of apples in:
a 3 trays　　**b** 5 trays　　**c** 10 trays.

2 Bottles of orange juice are sold in packs of 6.

Number of *b*ottles = **6** times number of *p*acks

Use this formula to find the number of bottles in:
a 4 packs　　**b** 10 packs　　**c** 20 packs.

Example　Lizzy is making pentagons.

The formula for pentagons can be written

number of *m*atchsticks = **5** × number of *p*entagons

Use the formula to find the number of matchsticks needed for **10** pentagons

number of matchsticks $= 5 \times 10$
$$= 50$$

---

3 Use the pentagon formula to find the number of matchsticks needed for:
a 6 pentagons　　**b** 8 pentagons　　**c** 20 pentagons.

4 Rolls are sold in packs of 8.

Number of *r*olls = **8** × number of *p*acks

Use this formula to find the number of rolls in:

a 5 packs   **b** 10 packs   **c** 20 packs.

5 Tennis balls are sold in cans of 3.

Number of *t*ennis balls = **3** × number of *c*ans

Use this formula to find the number of tennis balls in:

a 4 cans   **b** 8 cans   **c** 20 cans.

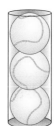

◄◄REPLAY► ►

For some formulas you will need 2 robots.

Example

$$3 \longrightarrow \boxed{\times 2} \longrightarrow 6 \longrightarrow \boxed{+1} \longrightarrow 7$$

Exercise 4 : 7

1 You will need copies of these robot screens. Complete the screens.

a
$$4 \longrightarrow \boxed{\times 2} \longrightarrow ? \longrightarrow \boxed{+1} \longrightarrow ?$$

b
$$6 \longrightarrow \boxed{\times 3} \longrightarrow ? \longrightarrow \boxed{+2} \longrightarrow ?$$

c
$$5 \longrightarrow \boxed{-1} \longrightarrow ? \longrightarrow \boxed{\times 2} \longrightarrow ?$$

d
$$3 \longrightarrow \boxed{\times 4} \longrightarrow ? \longrightarrow \boxed{+2} \longrightarrow ?$$

Formulas using two robots

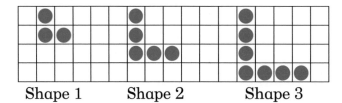

Shape 1   Shape 2   Shape 3

The results for Steve's **L** shapes were:

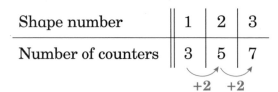

Shape number	1	2	3
Number of counters	3	5	7

+2   +2

The rule +2 suggests ×2 is something to do with the formula.

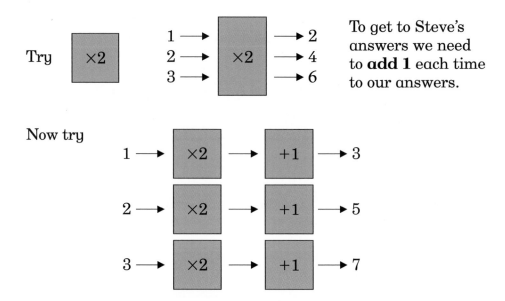

Try   ×2

1 ⟶   ⟶ 2
2 ⟶   ×2   ⟶ 4
3 ⟶   ⟶ 6

To get to Steve's answers we need to **add 1** each time to our answers.

Now try

1 ⟶ ×2 ⟶ +1 ⟶ 3

2 ⟶ ×2 ⟶ +1 ⟶ 5

3 ⟶ ×2 ⟶ +1 ⟶ 7

The formula is:

Shape number ⟶ ×2 ⟶ +1 ⟶ Number of counters

Finding the first part of the formula

From your table find the rule.
This is the number that you multiply by in your formula.

Exercise 4:8

W7 **1**

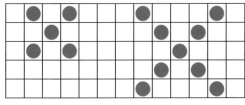

Shape 1   Shape 2

Use Steve's table for his **X** shapes to answer the questions.

Shape number	1	2	3	4
Number of counters	5	9	13	17

? ? ?

a The rule is ...

b The first part of the formula will be   ×?

c Try the first part of the formula in the machine.

Steve's answers

1 ⟶   ⟶ ...   5
2 ⟶   ×?   ⟶ ...   9
3 ⟶   ⟶ ...   13
4 ⟶   ⟶ ...   17

d To get Steve's answers we need to add ... each time.

e Now try:

1 ⟶ ×? ⟶ +? ⟶
2 ⟶ ×? ⟶ +? ⟶
3 ⟶ ×? ⟶ +? ⟶
4 ⟶ ×? ⟶ +? ⟶

f The formula is:

Shape number ⟶ ×? ⟶ +? ⟶ Number of counters

W8 **2**

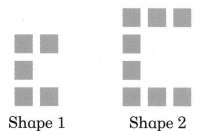

Shape 1   Shape 2

Use the table for ⊏ shapes to answer the questions.

Shape number	1	2	3	4
Number of counters	5	8	11	14

a The rule is …

b The first part of the formula will be [×?]

c Try the first part of the formula in the machine.

d To get the number of counters we need to add … each time.

e The formula is:

Shape number → [×?] → [+?] → Number of counters

W9 **3** Find the formula to work out the number of matchsticks needed for each shape.

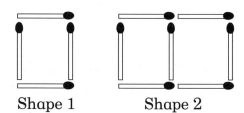

Shape 1   Shape 2

Shape number	1	2	3	4
Number of matchsticks	4	7	10	13

1 Alan is making octagons with matchsticks.

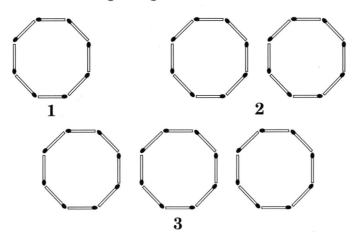

1 **2**

3

a Count the number of matchsticks in each diagram.
Put your results in a table.

Number of octagons	1	2	3	4
Number of matchsticks	8			32

+? +? +?

Copy and complete:

b Each shape uses ... more matchsticks than the one before.

c The rule is: add ... extra matchsticks each time.

2 Write down the **rule** for each number pattern and the next **two** numbers.

a 2, 4, 6, 8

b 4, 8, 12, 16

c 10, 13, 16, 19

d 25, 30, 35, 40

3 Write down the rule that belongs on each robot screen.

a 3 ⟶ ? ⟶ 9

b 5 ⟶ ? ⟶ 8

4 Find one rule which fits **both** robot screens.

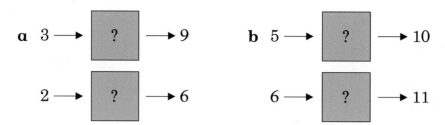

5 Alex makes some shapes using counters.

Alex counts the number of counters
he has used each time.
His results are in the table below.

Shape number	1	2	3	4
Number of counters	5	10	15	20

+? +? +?

a How many extra counters has he used each time?

b Find the robot that will fit any shape number

```
1 ——→        ——→ 5
2 ——→   ?    ——→ 10
3 ——→        ——→ 15
4 ——→        ——→ 20
```

c Write the formula using a robot.

6 Eggs are sold in boxes of 6.

number of **e**ggs = **6** × number of **b**oxes

Use this formula to find the number of eggs in:

a 5 boxes   **b** 10 boxes   **c** 20 boxes.

5 Transformations

QUESTIONS

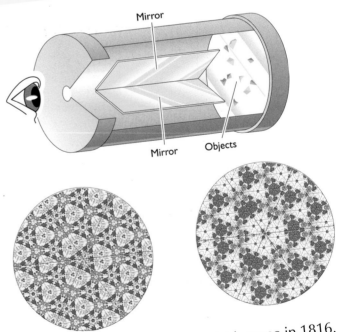

David Brewster, invented the kaleidoscope in 1816. It is made with two mirrors in a tube. The angle between the mirrors can be 45° or 60°. When the end of the tube is rotated, coloured pieces of plastic between the two mirrors are reflected to make symmetrical patterns.

Which other angles would work? Why?

1 Reflections

The lake acts like a mirror.
The trees are reflected in it.
The mirror line is a line of
symmetry.

◀◀REPLAY▶

Exercise 5 : 1

Copy each diagram on to squared paper.
Draw its reflection in the mirror line.
You can use tracing paper or a mirror to help you.

H 1

1

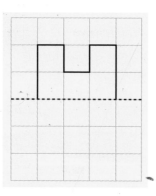

3

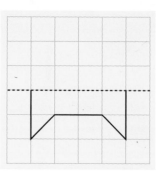

2

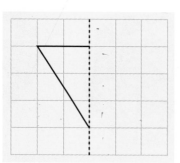

4

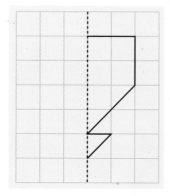

Copy each diagram on to squared paper.
Draw its reflection in the mirror line.
You can use tracing paper or a mirror to help you.

2 **5** 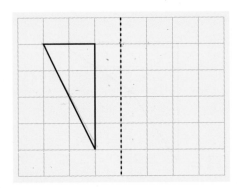 **8**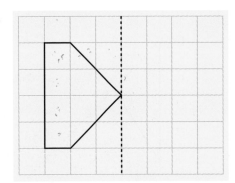

6 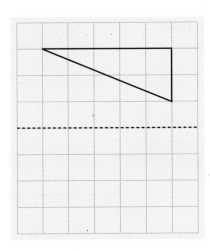 **9**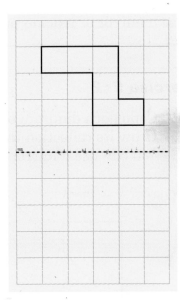

7 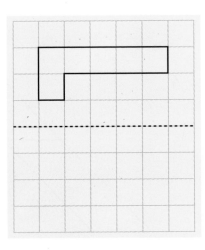 **10**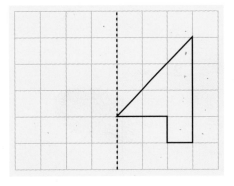

3

5

The mirror line is not always horizontal or vertical.

This mirror line is **diagonal**.

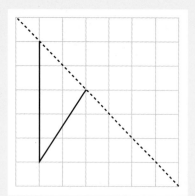 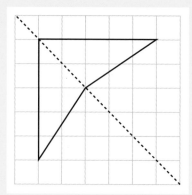

Use a mirror or tracing paper to help you.

Exercise 5:2

Copy each diagram on to squared paper.
Draw its reflection in the mirror line.
You can use a mirror or tracing paper to help you.

H 4

1
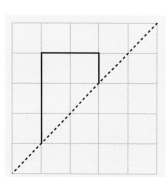

3
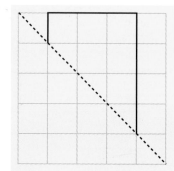

2
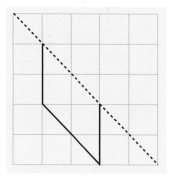

4
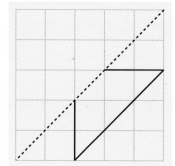

84

This shape is made from cubes.
It has reflection symmetry.

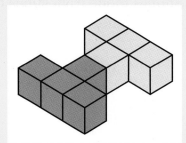

It can be divided into two
identical pieces.
This means that they are
the same shape.

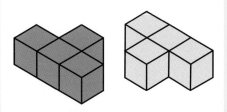

Exercise 5:3

You need some cubes.
Make each shape.
Divide each shape into two identical pieces.

1

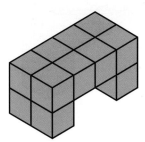

2

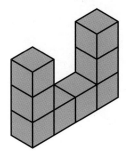

3

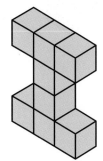

4

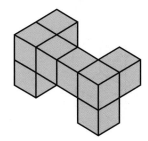

Shapes made from cubes can be drawn more easily on triangular dotty paper.

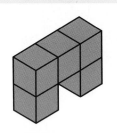

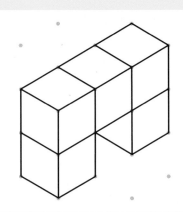

Make sure your paper is this way up.

Make each shape.
Draw it on triangular dotty paper.
Stick it in your book.

5

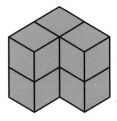

7

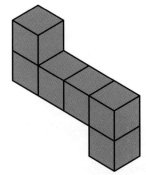

6

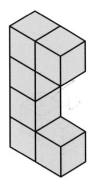

8

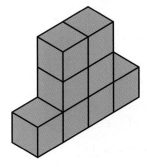

 5

86

2 Translation

As the ducks move in a straight line they look the same.

Translation	A **translation** is a movement in a straight line.
Translation symmetry	**Translation symmetry** is when a shape looks the same as it moves in a straight line.

Example

Make a translation 3 squares left.

Draw a square.
Mark a dot on a corner.
Move the dot 3 squares left.
Draw the new square.

You can make translations
up, **down**, **left** or **right**.

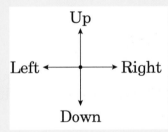

Exercise 5:4

You need squared paper.

1 Draw a square.
    Make a translation 5 squares right.

2 Draw a square.
    Make a translation 3 squares up..

3 Draw a square.
    Make a translation 4 squares left.

4 Draw a square.
    Make a translation 1 squares down.

Example

Colour the shape red.

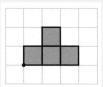

Choose a point to help you.
Make a translation
5 squares right.
Draw the shape in its new position.
Colour the shape blue.

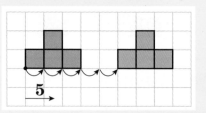

You need squared paper.

H 6

5 Copy this shape.
Colour it red.
Choose a point.
Make a translation 4 squares right.
Colour the new shape blue.

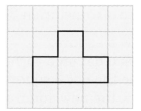

6 Copy this shape.
Colour it red.
Choose a point.
Make a translation 5 squares down.
Colour the new shape blue.

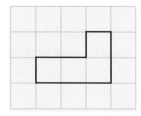

7 Copy this shape.
Colour it red.
Choose a point.
Make a translation 6 squares left.
Colour the new shape blue.

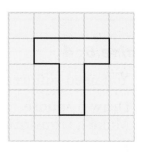

8 Copy this shape.
Colour it red.
Choose a point.
Make a translation 3 squares up.
Colour the new shape blue.

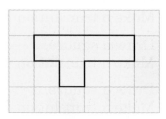

Example

Roy makes two translations of one shape.
He moves it 4 squares right then 3 squares down.

Colour the shape red.
Choose a point.
Make a translation 4 squares right.

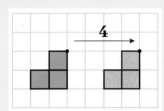

Make a translation 3 squares down.

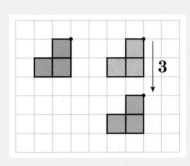

Colour the new shape blue.

You need squared paper.

9 Copy this shape.
Choose a point.
Make a translation 2 squares right
then 3 squares up.
Colour the new shape blue.

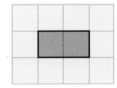

10 Copy this shape.
Choose a point.
Make a translation 4 squares left
then 1 square up.
Colour the new shape blue.

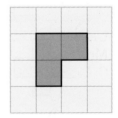

11 Copy this shape.
Choose a point.
Make a translation 3 squares right
then 3 squares down.
Colour the new shape blue.

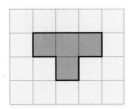

12 Copy this shape.
Choose a point.
Make a translation 5 squares left
then 2 squares down.
Colour the shape blue.

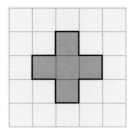

G 1, 2
3, 4

Example   Roy has drawn a translation.
Work out the translation he made.

Choose a point.

Count across first:
5 right.

Count down next:
3 down.

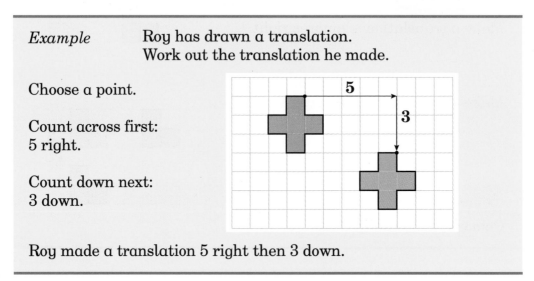

Roy made a translation 5 right then 3 down.

Exercise 5:5

Write down the two translations for each red shape.
Count right or left then up or down.

H 8

1
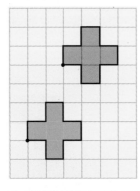

3
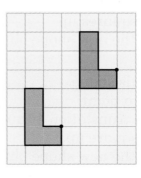

2
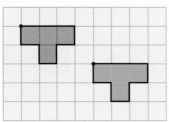

4
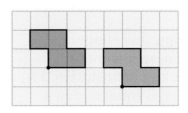

H 9

3 Rotation

This is a pelton wheel.
It moves water by turning.
As it turns it looks the same
in different positions.

Rotation	A **rotation** is a turning movement round in a circle.
Rotational symmetry	A shape has **rotational symmetry** if it fits on top of itself more than once as it makes a complete turn.
Order of rotational symmetry	The **order of rotational symmetry** is the number of times that the shape fits on top of itself. This must be 2 or more.

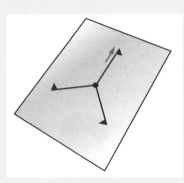

Lydia traces this shape onto
tracing paper.
She marks the centre with a dot.
This is the **centre** of rotational
symmetry.
She draws an arrow pointing up.

Lydia rotates the tracing paper over the picture.
It looks the same in 3 positions.

This shape has rotational symmetry, order 3.

Exercise 5:6

All these shapes have rotational symmetry.
Write down the order of rotational symmetry.
Use tracing paper to help you.

1

A Viking shield
from the front.

3

An umbrella seen
from the top.

5

The sails of a
windmill from
the front.

2

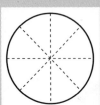

A slice of lemon.

4

A slice of star fruit.

6

A car wheel
from the side.

Tariq makes his own pattern with rotational symmetry, order 8.

(1) Fold a circle into 8.

(2) Cut out one section.

(3) Draw a design.
Cut it out.

(4) Draw a circle the
same size as
before. Use the
design as a
stencil. Draw
round it eight
times on your circle to make a
rotational symmetry pattern.

Make your own rotational symmetry patterns.

4 Enlargement

Under the magnifying glass
the letters are 3 times bigger.

Enlargement   An **enlargement** changes the size of an object.
The change is the same in all directions.

Example   Tariq wants to make his initials 2 times bigger.

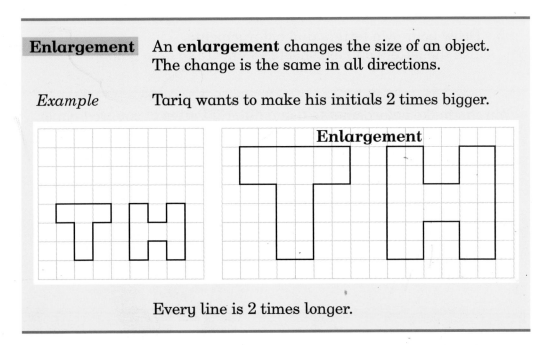

Every line is 2 times longer.

Exercise 5 : 7

You need squared paper.

 12, 13

1 Copy the letter.
Draw it 2 times bigger.

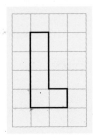

2 Copy the letter.
Draw it 2 times bigger.

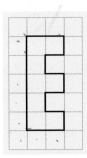

3 Copy the letter.
Draw it 3 times bigger.

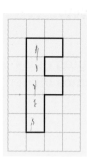

4 Copy the letter.
Draw it 3 times bigger.

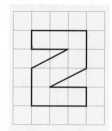

 14, 15

H 16

5 Draw your own letters and enlargements.
Use the letters on Helpsheets 14 and 15 to help you.

W 2

You can make enlargements using different sizes of squared paper.
Toby and Matthew go to the same school.
Matthew makes a 2 times enlargement of his badge.

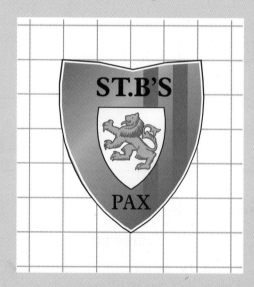

1 Make your own 2 times enlargement of their school badge.

To make a 4 times enlargement Toby uses 2 cm squared paper.

2 Make your own 4 times enlargement of their badge.
Use 2 cm squared paper.

3 Use different sizes of squared paper to make your own designs
and enlargements.

H 17   Copy these diagrams on to squared paper.
Draw their reflections in the mirror lines.
You can use tracing paper or a mirror to help you.

1
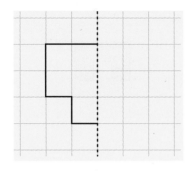

4
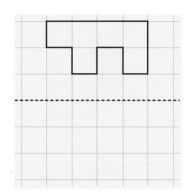

2
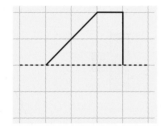

5
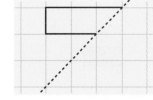

3
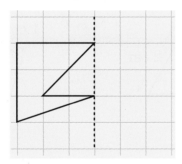

6
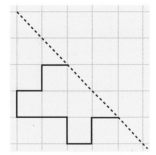

You need squared paper.

7   Draw a square.
Make a translation 2 squares up.

8   Draw a square.
Make a translation 3 squares left.

9 Copy this shape.
Colour it red. Choose a point.
Make a translation
3 squares down.

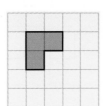

10 Copy this shape.
Colour it blue. Choose a point.
Make a translation
4 squares right.

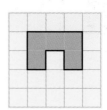

11 Copy this shape.
Colour it red. Choose a point.
Make a translation 3 squares
left then 2 squares down.

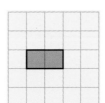

12 Copy this shape.
Colour it blue. Choose a point.
Make a translation 4 squares
right then 1 square up.

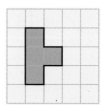

13 Write down the order of rotational symmetry of these shapes.

a

b

c

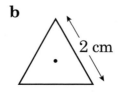

You need squared paper.

14 Copy the shape.
Draw it 2 times bigger.

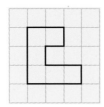

15 Copy the shape.
Draw it 3 times bigger.

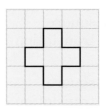

6 Don't be negative!

QUESTIONS

The coldest place in the world is the Pole of Inaccessibility in Antarctica. Its annual mean temperature is −58°C.

Braemar, in Scotland, is the coldest weather station in the UK. Its annual mean temperature is 6.3°C. On cold nights, Braemar has had temperatures down to −27°C

The lowest temperature possible is absolute zero, 0 K on the Kelvin scale or −273.15°C. The lowest temperature reached on Earth is 0.000 000 000 28 K. This was at the Low Temperature Laboratory of Helsinki University, Finland, in February 1993.

1 ◀◀ REPLAY ▶

You have already met negative numbers.

Negative numbers	**Negative numbers** are less than nought and have a − sign in front. For example, −4, −8, −20
Positive numbers	**Positive numbers** are greater than nought and sometimes have a + sign in front. For example, 4, +8, 20
Nought	**Nought** is neither negative nor positive. It can be called 0, zero, nothing or nil.

Exercise 6 : 1

1   6   −3   0   −5   +2   −1   +7   9

    a Write down the negative numbers.

    b Write down the positive numbers.

    c Which number is left? Why is it left?

Look at this thermometer scale.

Examples

1°C is lower than 4°C

−2°C is lower than 1°C

−4°C is lower than −1°C

3°C is higher than 2°C

1°C is higher than −2°C

−1°C is higher than −3°C

H 1

2 Which temperature is lower?

a −2°C or 4°C

b 0°C or −5°C

c −2°C or −5°C

G 1, 2

3 Which temperature is higher?

a −6°C or 1°C

b −1°C or 0°C

c −3°C or −4°C

4 Put these temperatures in order, lowest first.

a −4°C, 5°C, −2°C, 3°C

b 5°C, −3°C, 0°C, −2°C, 7°C

c −6°C, 1°C, −1°C, −3°C, 0°C, 4°C

5 Put these temperatures in order, highest first.

a −1°C, 2°C, −3°C

b −2°C, 5°C, 1°C, −1°C, 2°C

c −10°C, 8°C, −5°C, −9°C, 2°C, −1°C

Number line   A **number line** has numbers placed in order.
You can put any numbers on a number line.

Stevie has 3 number cards.
She puts them on her number line.

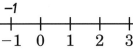

She writes the
numbers in order,
smallest first.

```
                    -2  -1           4
   +---+---+---+---+---+---+---+---+---+---+
  -5  -4  -3  -2  -1   0   1   2   3   4   5
```

−2, −1, 4

Exercise 6:2

1 **1 a** Put 3, −2, 0 on a number line.
   b Write the numbers in order, smallest first.

1 **2 a** Put −3, 5, −1 on a number line.
   b Write the numbers in order, smallest first.

1 **3 a** Put 4, 2, −1 on a number line.
   b Write the numbers in order, smallest first.

1 **4 a** Put −4, −3, −5 on a number line.
   b Write the numbers in order, smallest first.

1 **5 a** Put −1, 0, −2, −4, 2 on a number line.
   b Write the numbers in order, smallest first.

2 **6** Write these numbers in order, smallest first.
   You can use a number line to help you.

   a −1, −2, −4, −3, −5   **c** 7, 0, −14, +8, −3

   b −3, 0, −5, 2, 3   **d** −10, +20, −15, −25, +30

2 **7** Write these numbers in order, highest first.
   You can use a number line to help you.

   a −4, −3, −5, −1, −2   **c** −8, 14, 0, +4, −13

   b −4, 0, −2, 3, 4   **d** −20, +10, −25, −5, +20

Example   What is the difference between these two temperatures?

−4°C   +2°C

Mark the temperatures on a thermometer.

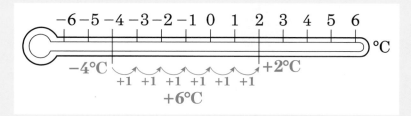

The difference is 6°C.

H 3, 4

8   What is the difference between these temperatures?

    a −1°C   3°C   **c** −6°C   0°C

    b −3°C   6°C   **d** −5°C   3°C

Example   You can use a number line to find the difference between two numbers.

Find the difference between −20 and +10.

Mark the numbers on the number line.

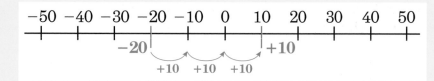

Count on to find the difference.

The difference is 30.

H 2

9   Find the difference between these numbers.
Use a number line to help you.

    a −15   −5   **d** −8   12

    b −25   5   **e** −1   17

    c −10   15   **f** −19   5

2 Money

Charlene is buying a peach.

The peach costs 27 p.

Charlene has the correct money. She gives the greengrocer a 20 p, a 5 p and a 2 p.

Exercise 6:3

H5

1 Write these amounts in words.

a 50 p	**d** 5 p	**g** £1
b 20 p	**e** 2 p	**h** £5
c 10 p	**f** 1 p	**i** £10

2 Write these coins in figures.
Add them up without a calculator.

a 1 twenty pence, 1 ten pence, 2 five pence

b 2 twenty pence, 1 five pence, 1 two pence

c 1 fifty pence, 2 ten pence, 1 five pence

d 1 fifty pence, 1 twenty pence, 1 ten pence

e 2 twenty pence, 3 five pence

f 2 fifty pence, 1 twenty pence

g 1 fifty pence, 1 twenty pence, 3 ten pence

Finding the change

Roy buys a pencil for 20 p.

He pays with a 50 p.

He finds the change by **counting on** from 20p to 50p.

He gets 30p change.

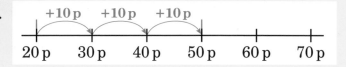

 3 Find the change in each question.
You can use a money number line to help you.

    a Dolly buys a pen for 30 p.
    She pays with a 50 p.

    b Belinda buys a pencil sharpener for 10 p.
    She pays with a 50 p.

    c Abigail buys some crisps for 25 p.
    She pays with a 50 p.

    d Alan buys an apple for 14 p.
    He pays with a 50 p.

    e Lynne buys a newspaper for 32 p.
    She pays with a 50 p.

4 In each question find the change from 50 p.

    a 5p   **f** 12p

    b 25p   **g** 33p

    c 35p   **h** 41p

    d 45p   **i** 28p

    e 30p   **j** 9p

5 Find the pairs of amounts that add together to make 50 p.

    17p 22p 33p 9p 35p 15p 28p 41p

H7 **6** Find the change in each question.
You can use a money number line to help you.

a Neil buys an eraser for 30 p.
He pays with £1.

b Denise buys a drink for 40 p.
She pays with £1.

c Holly buys a toy for 60 p.
She pays with £1.

d Sam buys a ball for 80 p.
He pays with £1.

e Elizabeth buys a notebook for 75 p.
She pays with £1.

f Jane buys a mirror for 85 p.
She pays with £1.

G4

H7 **7** In each question find the change from £1.

a 50 p		**f** 91 p
b 25 p		**g** 72 p
c 20 p		**h** 63 p
d 95 p		**i** 19 p
e 35 p		**j** 27 p

G5, 6 **8** Find the pairs of amounts that add together to make £1.
19 p   34 p   47 p   81 p   8 p   66 p   92 p   53 p

Mark's school has a shop that sells stationery.

These are the prices:

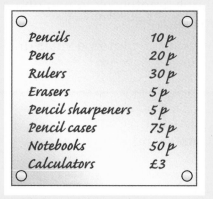

Pencils	10 p
Pens	20 p
Rulers	30 p
Erasers	5 p
Pencil sharpeners	5 p
Pencil cases	75 p
Notebooks	50 p
Calculators	£3

Pupils take it in turns to help at the shop.
When they sell something they fill out
an order sheet.
Mark has just sold 2 pencils, a pen and
a ruler to Khalid.
He writes them on the pad and adds
them up.

They cost 70 p.

Khalid pays with £1.

Mark gives him 30 p change.

School Order Pad

Number/Item	Price
2 pencils	20p
1 pen	20p
1 ruler	30p
Total	70p

Exercise 6:4

 8

1 Fill out an order sheet for each sale. Use the list of prices
from Mark's school shop.
Write down the change for each purchase.

a Steven buys a ruler and a pencil. He pays with 50 p.

b Kyle buys a pencil, a pen and a pencil sharpener.
He pays with 50 p.

c Amber buys a notebook and a ruler. She pays with £1.

d Mirae buys an eraser, a pencil sharpener and 2 pencils.
She pays with £1.

e Sui Yuk buys a pencil case, an eraser, a pencil
sharpener and a pencil. He pays with £1.

f Alice buys 3 pens, 2 pencils and a notebook.
She pays with £2.

g Laura buys a notebook, a pen and a calculator.
She pays with £5.

h Nigel buys a calculator, a ruler and 3 pencils.
He pays with £5.

Example

Fergus has 50 p to spend on stationery.

He could buy a ruler and 2 pencils.
30 p + 10 p + 10 p does not go over 50 p.

$$\begin{array}{r} 30p \\ + \\ 10p \\ + \\ 10p \\ \hline 50p \end{array}$$

---

2 Work out which of these Fergus could buy and which he could not buy with 50 p. Use the list of prices from Mark's school shop.

a A ruler, a pencil and an eraser.

b A ruler, 3 pencils and a pen.

c A pencil sharpener, 2 pens and a pencil.

d An eraser, a pen and 4 pencils.

3 Work out which of these Paula could buy and which she could not buy with £1. Use the list of prices from Mark's school shop.

a A notebook, a ruler and a pencil.

b A ruler and a pencil case.

c A pencil case, a pen and a pencil.

d A pencil case, an eraser, a pencil sharpener and a pencil.

The school sells snacks at break time in the tuck shop.

Hitesh buys a beefburger and a packet of mints.

The cost is

$$\begin{array}{r} 65\,p \\ + 19\,p \\ \hline 84\,p \end{array}$$

He pays with £1. He gets 16 p change.

Crisps	25 p	Doughnuts	28 p
Toffees	34 p	Beefburger	65 p
Mints	19 p	Samosa	32 p

4 Find the cost of each purchase.
   Write down the change for each one.

a Charlotte buys a doughnut.
   She pays with £1.

b Della buys a samosa.
   She pays with £1.

c Viv buys a packet of toffees.
   She pays with £1.

d Angela buys a packet of
   mints and a packet of crisps.
   She pays with £1.

e Karen buys 2 samosas.
   She pays with £1.

f Barbara buys 3 packets of toffees.
   She pays with £2.

g Patrick buys 2 doughnuts and
   a beefburger.
   He pays with £2.

h Adrian buys 2 packets of crisps
   and a beefburger.
   He pays with £2.

i John buys 3 beefburgers.
   He pays with £5.

j Jim buys a packet of mints and
   a doughnut. He pays with £5.

3   The calculator

◄◄ REPLAY ►

Example

Katie is adding 72 p and 13 p using a calculator.

She keys in:

| 7 | 2 | + | 1 | 3 | = |

The display shows 85.

85.

This is 85 p.

Exercise 6:5

1   Use your calculator to find the answers to these questions.
Check your answers by doing the sums in your book.

    a   24 p + 53 p   **e**   43 p + 49 p

    b   19 p + 66 p   **f**   25 p + 69 p

    c   52 p + 27 p   **g**   25 p + 58 p

    d   22 p + 78 p   **h**   69 p + 53 p

Reading the calculator display

Josie has added some money on her calculator.
She keyed the amounts in in pounds.

 0.72   This display is £0.72   0.6   This display is £0.60

 1.28   This display is £1.28   7.5   This display is £7.50

2 These are answers to money calculations.
Each one was keyed in in pounds.
Write down the answer in money.

a [0.86]   e [1.84]

b [0.41]   f [7.63]

c [0.2]   g [4.5]

d [0.8]   h [12.7]

Adding the cost of your shopping with a calculator

Jason buys a chicken for £3.45 and some carrots for £1.28.

He keys the amounts into his calculator like this:

[3][.][4][5][+][1][.][2][8][=]

He writes down the answer from his calculator.   [4.73]

The chicken and carrots cost £4.73.

---

3 Use your calculator to add up these amounts.
Write down the total cost.

a Chicken   £2.79
  Ice cream   £1.99

b Potatoes   £2.35
  Apples   £1.45
  Oranges   £1.25

c Cheese   £2.99
  Coffee   £1.85
  Milk   £1.09

d Biscuits   £1.20
  Pizza   £2.49
  Chips   £1.79

Adding pence and pounds with a calculator

Lester buys a packet of cereal costing £1.85 and a loaf of bread costing 66p.

He changes 66p to £0.66

He keys the amounts into his calculator like this:

| 1 | . | 8 | 5 | + | 0 | . | 6 | 6 | = |

He writes down the answer from his calculator. **2.51**

The cereal and bread cost £2.51.

4 Use your calculator to add up these amounts.
Write down the total cost.

a Bread 76p
Rice £1.69

c Spaghetti £1.58
Tomatoes 49p
Newspaper 45p
Soap powder £4.98

b Tinned beans 46p
Bread 68p
Potatoes £2.82

d Drinks £1.29
Meat £3.47
Shampoo £1.88
Matches 56p

(G)7, 8

5 David bought 3 items from this list. They cost £2.35 altogether.
Use your calculator to work out which items he bought.
Write them down.

Soap	Margarine	Bread	Sugar	Milk
77p	£1.29	53p	75p	31p

6 Rachel bought 3 items from this list.
They cost £3.55 altogether.
Use your calculator to work out
which items she bought.
Write them down.

Magazine	£2.50
Hair spray	£1.99
Apples	58p
Flour	47p
Fish	£1.22

1 −1 +2 −4 −2 5 +3 0 −6

    a Write down the negative numbers.

    b Write down the positive numbers.

    c Which number is left?
       Why is it left?

2 Which temperature is lower?

    a −1°C or 3°C   **b** 2°C or 0°C   **c** −3°C or −6°C

3 Put these temperatures in order, lowest first.

    a −2°C, 4°C, −5°C, 3°C

    b 1°C, 0°C, −2°C, −1°C, 4°C

4 Put these temperatures in order, highest first.

    a −3°C, 5°C, −1°C, 0°C

    b 6°C, −2°C, 5°C, −4°C, 7°C

5 What is the difference between these temperatures?

    a −2°C 1°C   **b** −4°C 3°C   **c** −3°C 2°C

6 Find the difference between these numbers?

    a −20 5   **b** −7 10   **c** −1 18

7 Write these coins in figures. Add them up without a calculator.

    a 1 twenty pence, 1 ten pence, 1 five pence

    b 1 fifty pence, 2 twenty pence, 1 two pence

    c 2 fifty pence, 1 twenty pence, 2 ten pence

    d 1 five pence, 1 two pence, 4 one pence

8 In each question find the change from 50 p.

    a 10 p   **d** 21 p

    b 15 p   **e** 19 p

    c 40 p   **f** 36 p

9 Find the cost in each question and then find the change from 50 p.

a 1 apple

b 2 oranges

c 2 apples

d 1 apple and 1 orange

e 3 apples

f 2 apples and 1 orange

10 In each question find the change from £1.

a 60 p

b 10 p

c 45 p

d 61 p

e 29 p

f 87 p

11 These are the answers to money calculations.
The amounts were keyed in in pounds.
Write down the answers in money.

a 0.32

b 7.25

c 6.2

e 1.11

f 0.5

g 18.6

12 Use your calculator to add up these amounts.
Write down the total cost.

a £2.36 + £1.25

b £1.51 + £0.80

c £0.50 + 65 p

d 20 p + 59 p

e £2.60 + 90 p

f £13.75 + 51 p

7 Angles

QUESTIONS

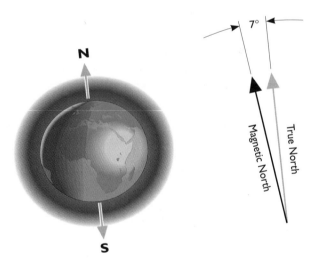

Compass needles point to *magnetic North*. This is slightly different from true North. Maps often have two arrows for North. One arrow is for true North and one is for magnetic North. Magnetic North should have a date by it because it varies from year to year! The angle between true North and Magnetic North is around 7°.

1   Types of angle

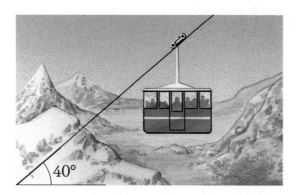

The cable car takes people up and down the mountain.
The angle with the ground must not be too large.

◄◄**REPLAY**► ►

Exercise 7 : 1

1   Trace the right angle.

Use *your* tracing paper right angle to check if *these* angles
are right angles.
Write down either: This is a right angle.
      or   This is bigger than a right angle.
      or   This is smaller than a right angle.

a   b   c

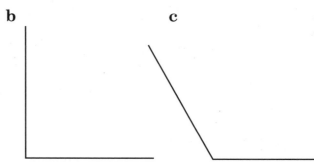

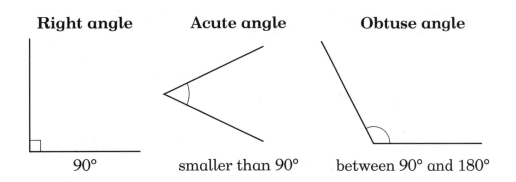

Right angle	Acute angle	Obtuse angle
90°	smaller than 90°	between 90° and 180°

Exercise 7:2

1 For each picture write down whether the angle marked is:

an acute angle

or a right angle

or an obtuse angle.

a

A pair of compasses

d

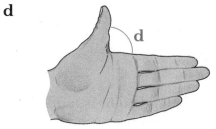

An outstretched thumb

b

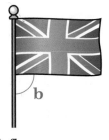

A flag

e

A see-saw

c

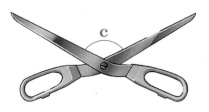

A pair of scissors

f

A pair of glasses

2 Measuring and drawing angles

Angles are measured in degrees.
The sign for degrees is °.
A protractor is used to measure angles.

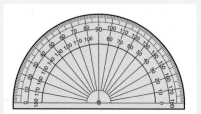 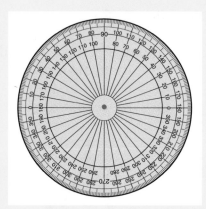

The mid point is marked in red.
The mid point must always be
placed on the point of the angle.

Example

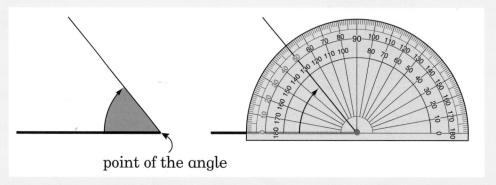

point of the angle

Make sure that the 0° line covers the dark arm of the angle.
Put your finger on 0°.
Now count round in 10 s
− 10°, 20°, 30°, 40°, 50°
− the angle is 50°.

Exercise 7:3

W 1
or
W 2

1 Measure this angle and the three others on the worksheet.

a 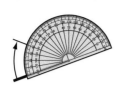 **or** **b**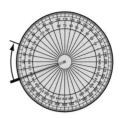

W 3

2 Measure the following angles using your protractor.
Put the 0° line on the dark arm of the angle.

a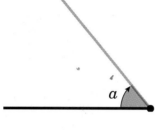

d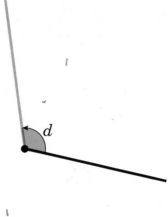

b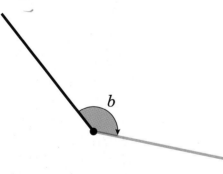

e

c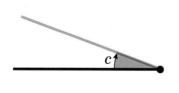

f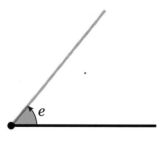

The protractor has 2 scales.
So far you have only needed
to use the **outside scale**.

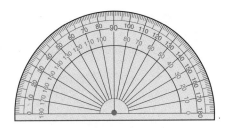

Look at the way the angles drawn below are being measured.

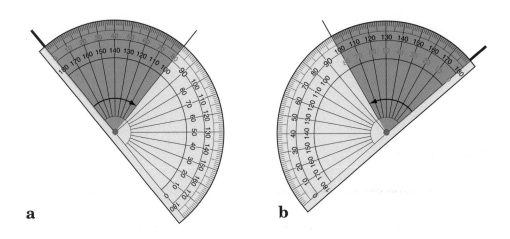

a **b**

The two angles are both the same   80°.

Angle *a* was measured using the **outside** scale.
Angle *b* was measured using the **inside** scale.

You must always use the scale that starts from zero.

Then count up in tens.

 4   **3** Measure the following angles using your protractor.
For these angles you will be using the inside scale.

a   **b**

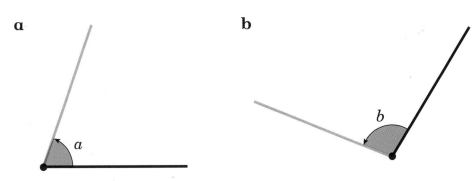

a   *b*

Example

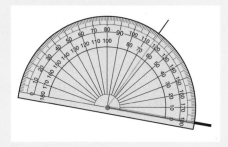

Chi Kit measures this angle.
He has to use the inside scale.
He starts at 0° and counts round
in tens.

10°, 20°, 30°, 40°, 50°, 60°

Chi Kit counts to 60°. He then
counts in ones, the small lines
marked after 60°.

1°, 2°, 3°, 4°

The angle is 64°.

Exercise 7:4

G 1, 2   Always estimate the size of an angle before you measure it.

W 5   **1**   Measure these angles using your protractor.
Place the 0° line on the dark arm.
For some angles you will need to use the outside scale,
for others the inside scale.

a

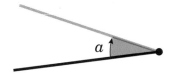

c

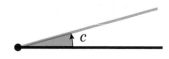

b

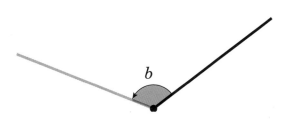

d

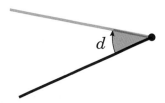

Drawing angles

Exercise 7:5

1 Follow the instructions below to draw an angle of 30°.

(1) Draw a line. Mark P at the end. ────────●P	(2) Put the mid point of the protractor on P. The 0° line must cover your line.
(3) Hold the protractor. Put your finger on 0° and count round in 10s. When you reach 30° put a mark. 	(4) Take away the protractor. Join the mark to the point P. Mark the angle and write in 30°. 30° ────────●P

2 Use this method to draw an angle of 60°.
  (i)   Draw a line and mark P at the end.
  (ii) Put the mid point of the protractor on P.
        The 0° line must cover your line.
  (iii) Put your finger on 0° and count round in 10 s to 60°.
  (iv) Make a mark at 60°.
  (v)   Take away the protractor and join the mark to the point P.
  (vi) Mark the angle and write in 60°.

3 In the same way draw the angles of: **a** 45°   **b** 120°   **c** 98°

3 Calculating with angles

∙∙

◀◀REPLAY▶ ▶

You do not always find angles by measuring.
You can calculate angles.

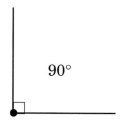

One right angle is 90°.

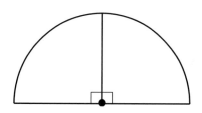

Two right angles make 180°.
Two right angles make half a turn.
This is a **straight line**.

The angles on a straight line always add up to 180°.

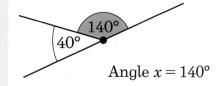

$150° + 30° = 180°$

Example   Find angle x.

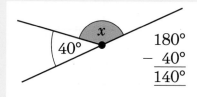

$$\begin{array}{r} 180° \\ -40° \\ \hline 140° \end{array}$$

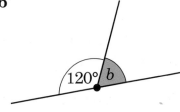

Angle $x = 140°$

Exercise 7:6

1 Find the angle marked with a letter.
Write the sum for each question.

   a   **b**

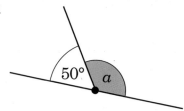

c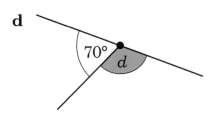

d

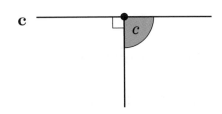

Exercise 7:7

W 6   Marie wants to find out if there is a rule for the total of the angles in a triangle.

Follow the instructions that
Marie was given to do this.

(1) Cut out the triangle.

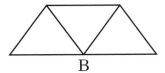

(2) Fold over the top corner T
to touch the base at B.

(3) Fold in the 2 sides so that the
points of the angles all meet at B.

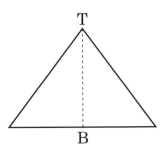

(4) Shade the 3 angles. Stick it in your book.
Together the 3 angles will make a straight line.
Angles on a straight line add up to 180 degrees.

(5) Copy this into your book:

> **Angles in a triangle add up to 180 degrees.**

Example   Find the angle marked with a letter.

The right
angle is 90°.

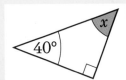

The given angles are 40° and 90°.
$$40° + 90° = 130°$$

Angle $x = 180° - 130°$
$$= 50°$$

Exercise 7:8

H 1

1 Calculate the size of the angles marked with a letter.
Write down your working.

a

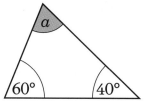

c

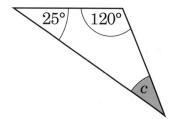

b

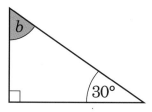

d

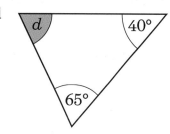

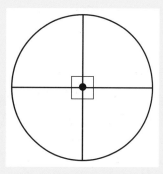

One right angle is 90°.

Four right angles make 360°.
This is a **full turn**.

Angles at a point make a full turn.
They add up to 360°.

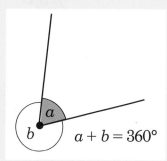

$a + b = 360°$

Example   Calculate angle *a*.

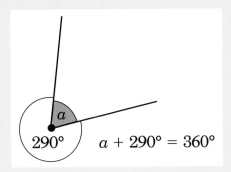

$a + 290° = 360°$

$a = 360° - 290°$

$$\begin{array}{r} 360° \\ - 290° \\ \hline 70° \end{array}$$

Angle $a = 70°$

Exercise 7:9

1 Calculate the angles marked with a letter.
Write down your working.

a

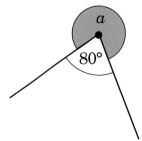

d

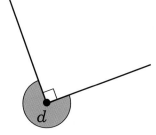

b

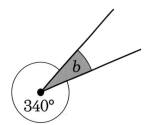

e

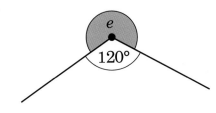

c

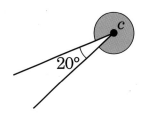

f

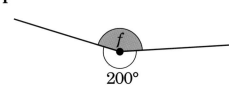

H 2

4 Parallel lines and polygons

The two lines of an angle meet
at a point called a **vertex**.

Some lines never meet.
They always stay the same distance apart.
These are called **parallel lines**.

Exercise 7:10

1 Draw or write down the names of 2 other things that
have parallel lines.

Example   Parallel lines on diagrams
are shown with arrows.

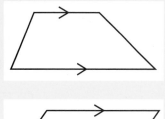

Two pairs of parallel lines
need extra arrows.

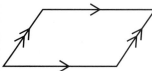

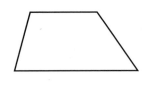 **2** On Worksheet 7 mark pairs of parallel sides with arrows, as in the examples.

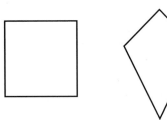

| **Polygons** | Flat shapes that have **all straight sides** and **no gaps** are called **polygons**. |

Exercise 7:11

 1 Which of these shapes are **polygons**?
Write down the answers in your book.

    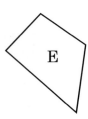

| **Regular polygons** | **Regular polygons** have:

All sides the same length.
All angles the same size.

Squares and equilateral triangles are **regular polygons**. |

square

equilateral triangle

2 Use your ruler to measure the sides of each of these shapes to find out which are regular polygons.
Write your answers in your book.

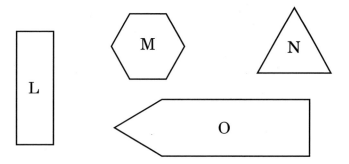

Naming polygons

There are special names given to polygons.
The name depends on the number of sides.

Number of sides	Name of polygon
3	triangle
4	quadrilateral
5	pentagon
6	hexagon
8	octagon

6 sides: hexagon

 There are some triangles and quadrilaterals that have special names.

Triangles

Scalene triangle   No equal sides.

Isosceles triangle   2 equal sides and 2 equal angles.

Equilateral triangle   3 equal sides and 3 equal angles.

Quadrilaterals

square

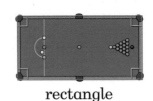
rectangle

kite

parallelogram

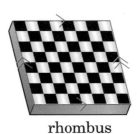
rhombus

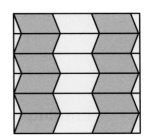
trapezium

W 7
W 8

3 Go back to Worksheet 7 and label each shape with its name. Choose from square, rectangle, rhombus, parallelogram, kite, trapezium.

Tessellations

A **tessellation** is a pattern made by repeating the same shape over and over again. There must not be any gaps in a tessellation.

Exercise 7 : 12

1 Look around inside and outside of the classroom.
Can you find a different shape that tessellates?
Draw a picture to show the shape you have found.
Repeat the shape 6 times to make a tessellation.

2

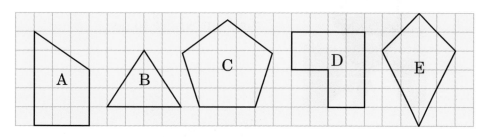

⬇ᴴ5, 6

4 of these shapes will tessellate.
1 shape will not tessellate.
Write down which shape will not tessellate.

⬇ᴴ7 **3** Bill and Elaine made tessellations for the classroom wall.

Bill used fish.   Elaine used cats.

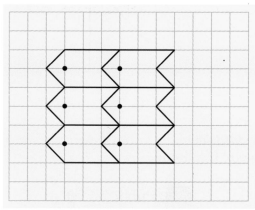 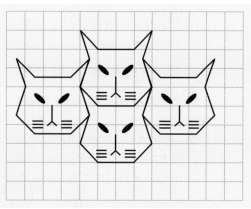

Do you need a display in your classroom?
Try a shape of your own or use Helpsheet 7.

5 Bearings

Simon is taking part in a treasure hunt. He uses a compass to find out where to go.

Exercise 7:13

 8

1 a Copy the compass diagram.

   North (N) and **east (E)** are marked.

   b Mark **south (S)** opposite north (N).
   Mark **west (W)** opposite east (E).

   c Mark **north east (NE)** between north and east.

   d Mark **south west (SW)** between south and west.

   e Mark **north west (NW)**.

   f Mark **south east (SE)**.

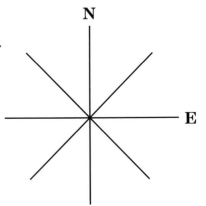

 9

2 Simon is practising using his compass.
   The map shows some places near his home.

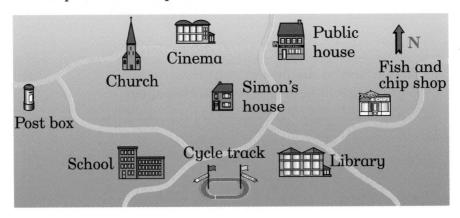

Starting from Simon's house each time, in which direction must Simon walk to get to:

a the fish and chip shop   **b** the cinema   **c** school?

What is Simon likely to take with him if he leaves his house and goes:

d south   **e** west   **f** south east?

Bearings	The direction in which you travel is called a **bearing**.

Bearings can also be measured in degrees.
Bearings are measured **clockwise** from **north**.
They are always written in 3 figures.

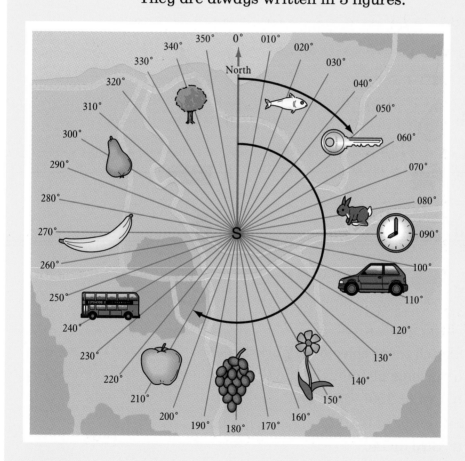

Before you can take a bearing the **north line** must be drawn from your starting point, S.

The **north line** has been drawn in red from S the starting point.

Example **a** Write down the bearing of the key from S.

The  is on the 050° line.

Its bearing is 050°.

b Write down the bearing of the apple from S.

The is on the 210° line.

Its bearing is 210°.

Exercise 7:14

1 Write down the bearing of these objects from S.

a   f

b   g

c   h

d   i

e   j

2 Sketch these objects on Worksheet 9.

   a Orange at 160°

   b Cat at 250°

   c Flower at 020°

   d Bird at 140°

   e Leaf at 350°

   f Lorry at 060°

   g Starfish at 100°

   h Strawberry at 280°

1

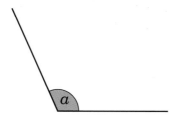
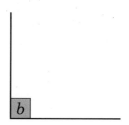
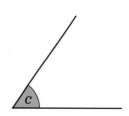

a Write down for each angle whether it is:

smaller than a right angle
or a right angle
or bigger than a right angle.

b Estimate the size of angle a.

c Estimate the size of angle c.

d Is angle c an acute angle or an obtuse angle?

W10 **2** Measure the following angles using a protractor.

a
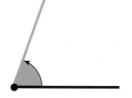

c
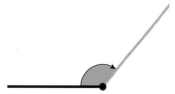

b
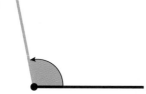

d

3 Draw the following angles.

a 40°   **b** 110°   **c** 25°   **d** 123°

4 **Calculate** the size of the angles marked with letters.
Do not measure them.
Write down the sum for each question.

a
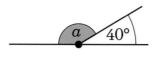

b
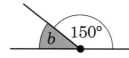

c
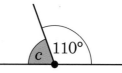

5   **Calculate** the size of the angles marked with a letter.
    Do not measure them.
    Write down the sum for each question.

a 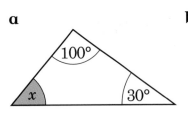   b 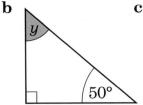   c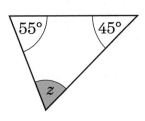

6   **a** How many degrees are there in a full turn?
    b Calculate the angles marked with a letter.

(1)   (2)   (3)

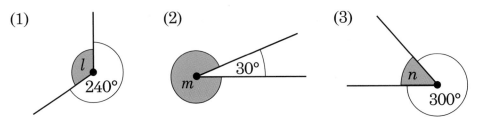

7   **a** Which of the shapes below are polygons?

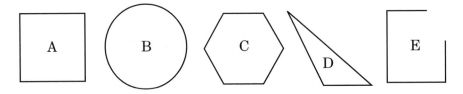

    b Write down the names of the shapes C and D.
    c Which of the polygons tessellate?

8   Give the three-figure bearings
    from point S of the objects
    marked on the diagram.

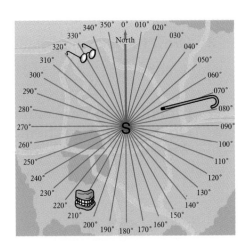

8 Probability

QUESTIONS

Every year about £525 million is paid in prizes by ERNIE.

ERNIE stands for Electronic Random Number Indicator Equipment. ERNIE picks the numbers of the winning Premium Bonds each month.

Each Premium Bond unit costs £1 and every unit has a 1 in 19 000 chance of winning a prize. Most prizes are £50 or £100 but there is a monthly prize of £1 million.

The chance of any Premium Bond unit winning the £1 million prize in any month is about 1 in 8 billion!

1 Probability scales

These pupils are using probability to help them decide what to say in the card game Higher or Lower.

◀◀REPLAY▶ ▶

Probability	**Probability** tells us how likely something is to happen.

We can show it on a probability scale.

An **impossible event** is one that will **never** happen.

A **certain event** is one that will **always** happen.

impossible ├─────────────────────────────┤ certain

Exercise 8:1

1 The following events are either impossible or certain.
Write impossible or certain for each statement.

   a You will live until you are 200 years old.

   b Spring comes before summer.

   c It will be dark tonight.

   d You will pass your driving test this year.

Not everything is impossible or certain.

The probability scale can be more detailed:

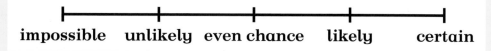

impossible   unlikely   even chance   likely   certain

W 1, 2

2 Place on a probability scale the following statements.

a A pig will fly.

b Christmas day will be on 25th December.
c You will get a present on your birthday.
d A coin thrown in the air will land tails up.
e It will snow in England in June.

3 These objects are dropped on to a floor.

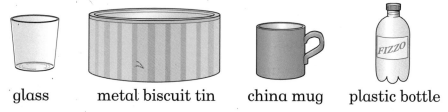

glass   metal biscuit tin   china mug   plastic bottle

List the objects in order of how likely they are to break.
Start with the **least** likely.

4 List the following football teams in order of how likely
they are to win the FA Cup.
Start with the **least** likely.

Man United   Station School   Exeter City   Man City

G 1, 2

2 Probability as fractions

Probabilities can be written as fractions.

In the questions on this page, sweets are picked without looking.

Kate has a bag of 8 sweets.

There is 1 orange sweet.
Kate has 1 chance out of 8 in picking an orange sweet.

The probability of Kate picking an orange sweet is $\frac{1}{8}$

Meg prefers green sweets. There are 3 green sweets.

The probability of Meg picking a green sweet is $\frac{3}{8}$

Exercise 8:2

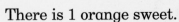

The pictures show the colours of sweets in three bags.

1 **a** Write down the number of jelly babies in the bag.

   b Write down the number of red sweets.

   c Write down the probability as a fraction of picking a red sweet.

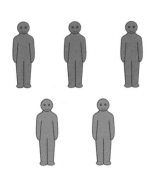

2 **a** Write down the number of Smarties in the bag.

   b Write down the number of yellow sweets.

   c Write down the probability as a fraction of picking a yellow sweet.

3 **a** Write down the probability of picking a black wine gum.

   b Write down the probability of picking a green wine gum.

Kate has made some spinners.
She has coloured the sections red and white.

This is her first spinner:

There are 6 sections altogether.
There are 2 red sections.
What is the probability of Kate getting red?

Kate has 2 chances out of 6 of getting red.

The probability of Kate getting red is $\dfrac{2}{6}$

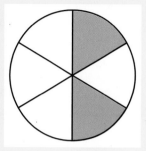

Exercise 8:3

1 Kate has made another spinner.

    a How many sections are there?

    b How many sections are red?

    c Write down the probability of
       Kate getting red.

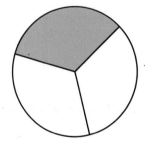

2 Kate has made 4 spinners.
  For each spinner write down the probability of Kate
  getting red.

    a

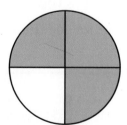

    c

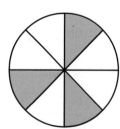

    b

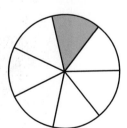

    d

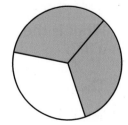

8

Fair	A **fair** game is one where each person has an equal chance of winning.

We often talk about a fair dice.

A fair dice is one which has an equal chance of landing on each number.

Throwing a 6-sided dice

Example   What is the probability of rolling an even number?

There are six numbers on a dice: 1, 2, 3, 4, 5, 6

There are three even numbers on a dice: 2, 4, 6

The probability of rolling an even number is $\dfrac{3}{6}$

3   Using a 6-sided dice, write down the probability of rolling

   a a 5

   b a 2

   c an odd number

   d a number less than 3 (a 1 or a 2)

   e a number less than 5

   f a number larger than 5.

Example   This is an 8-sided dice.

There are 8 numbers on the dice: 1, 2, 3, 4, 5, 6, 7, 8

What is the probability of rolling a 3?

The probability of rolling a 3 is $\dfrac{1}{8}$

4 Using an 8-sided dice, find the probability of rolling

  a a 2   **d** a number less than 3

  b a 7   **e** a number larger than 4

  c an even number   **f** 5 or more.

Using numbers for impossible and certain events

We can write impossible and certain events using numbers.

There are 5 red sweets in a bag.

It is **impossible** to choose a green sweet.

The probability of choosing

a green sweet is $\dfrac{0}{5}$

Using a calculator, $\dfrac{0}{5}$ is $\boxed{0} \div \boxed{5} = \boxed{0}$

The probability of choosing a green sweet is 0.

> **The probability of an impossible event is always 0.**

A sweet from the bag is **certain** to be red.

The probability of choosing a red sweet is $\dfrac{5}{5}$

Using a calculator, $\dfrac{5}{5}$ is $\boxed{5} \div \boxed{5} = \boxed{1}$

The probability of choosing a red sweet is 1.

> **The probability of a certain event is always 1.**

Impossible event – probability is 0

Certain event – probability is 1

Exercise 8:4

1 Draw this probability scale.

The following statements are either **impossible** or **certain**.

a A child running at 70 miles per hour.

b In each year November comes before December.

c A dog is born with 10 legs.

Write **a**, **b**, **c** on the probability scale at 0 or 1.

When we have worked out the probability of an event using numbers we can also show our answers on a probability scale.

Example Ian chooses a letter from the word T R E E S.

      a Write down the probability that he chooses an E.

      b Write down the probability that he chooses a Z.

      c Write E and Z in the correct place on the probability scale.

      a The probability that he chooses an E is $\frac{2}{5}$.

      b The probability that he chooses a Z is impossible, so it is 0.

      c On the probability scale:

Exercise 8:5

1 Robert chooses a letter from the word S C H O O L.

Write down the probability that he chooses:

a an L   **b** an O   **c** a P.

d Write L, O and P in the correct place on the probability scale.

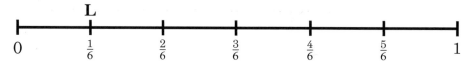

2 Sheila rolls a 6-sided dice.
Write down the probability of rolling

    a a 6   **c** a number less than 7

    b an even number   **d** an 8.

W 3   **e** Put **b**, **c**, **d** in the correct place on the probability scale.

3 Kelvin has 8 socks in his drawer.
5 are black, 2 are navy
and 1 is white.

Write down the probability
of Kelvin taking

    a a black sock

    b a navy sock

    c a white sock

    d a green sock.

W 3   **e** Write **b** for black, **n** for navy, **w** for white and **g** for green in the correct place on the probability scale.

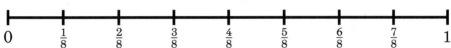

4 Justin has these 5 coins in his pocket.

Justin chooses one at random.

    a Write down the probability of Justin getting

        i a 5p coin   **iii** a £1 coin

        ii a 2p coin   **iv** a coin worth less than £1.

W 3   **b** Write 2p, 5p, £1 and 'less than £1' in the correct place on the probability scale.

G 3, 4

3 Expectation

We can work out expected results of experiments and games using probability.

A bag contains 8 red counters and 2 blue counters.

James picks a counter without looking.
He records the colour in a tally-table.
He puts the counter back.

James does this 10 times.
He expects to get

For every 8 red counters he would expect 2 blue ones.

James decides to do the experiment more times.

He does it 30 times.

For 10 turns, he expects to get 8 red counters and 2 blue counters.

For 30 turns

$$10 \longrightarrow \boxed{\times 3} \longrightarrow 30$$

he would expect to get

$$8 \longrightarrow \boxed{\times 3} \longrightarrow 24 \text{ red counters}$$

$$2 \longrightarrow \boxed{\times 3} \longrightarrow 6 \text{ blue counters}$$

Total 30 counters

Exercise 8:6

 4

1 a James decides to do the experiment **20 times**.
How many red and blue counters would he expect to get?

For 10 turns, he expects to get 8 red and 2 blue counters.
For 20 turns

$$10 \longrightarrow \boxed{\times 2} \longrightarrow 20$$

he would expect to get

$$8 \longrightarrow \boxed{\times 2} \longrightarrow \ldots\ldots \text{ red counters}$$

$$2 \longrightarrow \boxed{\ldots} \longrightarrow \ldots\ldots \text{ blue counters}$$

b James does the experiment again. He does it **50 times**.
How many red and blue counters would he expect to get?

For 10 turns, he expects to get 8 red and 2 blue counters.
For 50 turns

$$10 \longrightarrow \boxed{\times 5} \longrightarrow 50$$

he would expect to get

$$8 \longrightarrow \boxed{\ldots} \longrightarrow \ldots\ldots \text{ red counters}$$

$$2 \longrightarrow \boxed{\ldots} \longrightarrow \ldots\ldots \text{ blue counters}$$

James changes the counters in the bag.
This time he has 4 yellow counters and
1 green counter.

When he does the experiment 5 times
he would expect to get 4 yellow counters
and 1 green counter.

W 5   **2**   How many yellow and green counters would James expect if he
did the experiment

a   10 times?

For 5 turns, he expects to get 4 yellow counters and 1 green
counter.
For 10 turns

5 ⟶ | ×**2** | ⟶ 10

he would expect to get

◯ 4 ⟶ | ×**2** | ⟶ ......   yellow counters

● 1 ⟶ | ×**2** | ⟶ ......   green counters

b   15 times?

For 15 turns

5 ⟶ | ×**3** | ⟶ 15

he would expect to get

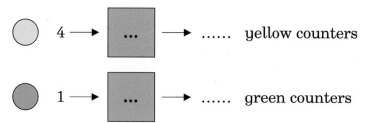

◯ 4 ⟶ | ... | ⟶ ......   yellow counters

● 1 ⟶ | ... | ⟶ ......   green counters

The more times you do these experiments the more likely you are to get the results you expect.

H 1 | **3** A bag contains 3 blue counters and 1 red counter.
Each time a counter is taken out, the colour is recorded and the counter is put back in the bag.

Copy the table and write in the missing answers.

When a counter is taken out

3	1
...	...
...	...

4 times we expect to get
8 times we expect to get
40 times we expect to get

W 6 | Try this experiment for yourself.

You need:
A paper bag
3 blue counters and 1 red counter

1. Pick a counter without looking.
2. Record the colour in a tally-table.
3. Put the counter back.

Write your results in a table.

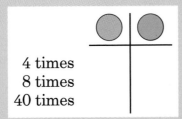

4 times
8 times
40 times

On Worksheet 6 bar-charts are drawn for the **expected** results.
Draw a bar for **your** results next to the bar for the expected ones.

Discuss your results with your teacher

4   Probability diagrams

MENU
Soup   99p
Fruit juice   60p

Fish fingers   £1.90
Sausages   £1.75
Veggie burger   £1.60
(all with chips and peas)

Sarah and Gavin are choosing their meal, a starter and a main course.

Sarah wants to know how many different meals she can choose.

She lists them in an organised way.

Starter	Main course
soup	fish fingers
soup	sausages
soup	veggie burger
juice	fish fingers
juice	sausages
juice	veggie burger

There are 6 possibilities. These are known as **outcomes**.

Exercise 8 : 7

1   a   Copy this table to show all of the possible meals from this menu. Fill it in.

Main course	Dessert

Main Courses
Chicken nuggets
Curry
Baked Potato

Dessert
Cake
Ice Cream

   b   Write down the number of outcomes.

2 Rapinder is having breakfast.
He must choose one drink and one cereal
from the menu.

  a Draw a table to show all his possible breakfasts.

Cereal	Drink

Cereals
Cornflakes
Coco Pops
Weetabix
Drinks
Tea
Coffee

  b Write down the number of outcomes.

3 Jennifer is deciding
what to wear.
She wants to wear
a T-shirt and a pair
of shorts.

  a Draw a table to show all the ways she could dress.

Colour of T-shirt	Colour of shorts

  b Write down the number of outcomes.

> Write down 3 of your favourite main courses and 2 of your favourite puddings.
>
> Draw a table to see how many different meals you could have.

4 Follow the instructions on Worksheet 7 (Aliens).

Example

Steven and Jane each have three cards, numbered 1, 2, and 3.

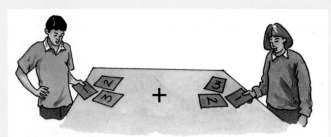

Steven picks up a blue card and Jane picks up a red card.
They **add** together the numbers on the two cards.

The table shows all the possible totals.
There are **9** possible outcomes.

		Jane		
+		1	2	3
Steven	1	2	3	4
	2	3	4	5
	3	4	5	6

a How many times was the total 3?

b What is the probability that the total is 3?

a The total 3 occurs in the table twice. The answer is 2.

b The number of 3s is 2.
The number of outcomes is 9.

So probability that the total is 3 is $\frac{2}{9}$.

Exercise 8:8

Look at the table in the example above.

1 a How many times is the total 4?

b Write down the probability that the total is 4.

2 a How many times is the total 5?

b Write down the probability that the total is 5.

3 **a** How many times is the total less than 5?

  b Write down the probability that the total is less than 5.

4 **a** How many times is the total greater than 1.

  b Write down the probability that the total is greater than 1.

Steven and Jane change their experiment.
This time they **multiply** the numbers on the two cards.

The table shows all the possible answers.

Jane			
×	1	2	3
1	1	2	3
Steven 2	2	4	6
3	3	6	9

Look at the table in the example above.

5 **a** How many times is the answer 3?

  b Write down the probability that the answer is 3.

6 **a** How many times is the answer an odd number?

  b Write down the probability that the answer is an odd number.

7 **a** How many times is the answer 5?

  b Write down the probability that the answer is 5.

8 **a** How many times is the answer less than 5?

  b Write down the probability that the answer is less than 5.

9 **a** How many times is the answer larger than 1?

  b Write down the probability that the answer is larger than 1.

9

1 Mark points **a**, **b** and **c** on the probability scale to show how likely you think each statement is.

   a A pregnant lady will give birth to a boy or a girl.

   b I will get an even number when I roll a 6-sided dice.

   c I can jump over a gate 20 metres high.

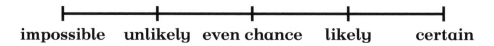

impossible   unlikely   even chance   likely   certain

2 What number represents the probability of an impossible event?

3 A bag of sweets contains 6 mints and 4 toffees.
Write down as a fraction the probability of choosing a mint.

4 Jo has made 3 spinners.
For each spinner write down the probability of Jo getting red.

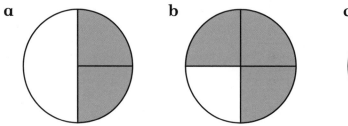
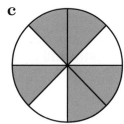

5 A 4-sided dice has numbers 1, 2, 3 and 4.
Write down the probability of rolling

   a a 3   **b** a 6   **c** a number less than 4.

9

6 Gill chooses a letter from the word   E V E N
Write down the probability as a fraction that she chooses:

   a N   **b** E   **c** X

   d Write N, E, X in the correct place on the probability scale.

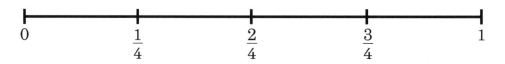

0             $\frac{1}{4}$ $\frac{2}{4}$ $\frac{3}{4}$ 1

3 **7** A bag contains 6 red counters and 2 blue counters.
Steve takes a counter without looking.
He records the colour in a tally-table.
He puts the counter back.

How many red and blue counters would he expect if he did the experiment 16 times?

Copy and fill in the gaps:

For 8 turns, he expects to get ... red counters and ... blue counters.

For 16 turns

$$8 \longrightarrow \boxed{\times \ldots} \longrightarrow 16$$

 $6 \longrightarrow \boxed{\times \ldots} \longrightarrow \ldots\ldots$ red counters

 $2 \longrightarrow \boxed{\times \ldots} \longrightarrow \ldots\ldots$ blue counters

 3 **8** Rachel is going to buy an ice cream.
She has the choice of 3 flavours of ice cream and 2 sauces.

vanilla   strawberry   chocolate

She decides to have one flavour of ice cream and some sauce.

Draw a table to show her different choices.

Ice cream	Sauce

9 Percentages and fractions

Which test mark is best?

1 Percentages

The Roman army had soldiers called centurions. They marched in a square of 10 soldiers by 10 soldiers.

Percentage	**Percentage** means out of 100. You write it like this % 13% means thirteen out of one hundred.

60 out of 100 centurions have red helmets.
60% have red helmets.

40 out of 100 centurions have blue helmets.
40% have blue helmets.

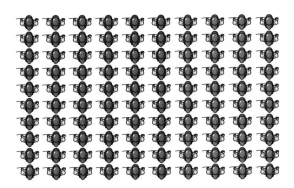

Exercise 9 : 1

1 **a** How many of the baseball players are wearing green hats?

b Write this in words out of one hundred.

c Write this as a percentage.

d How many baseball players have yellow hats?

e Write this in words out of one hundred.

f Write this as a percentage.

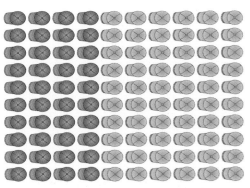

2 a How many light bulbs are there altogether?

b How many bulbs are on?

c What percentage are on?

d How many light bulbs are off?

e What percentage are off?

60% of helmets were red and 40% of helmets were blue.
   60% + 40% = 100%

40% of hats were green and 60% of hats were yellow.
   40% + 60% = 100%

10% of bulbs were on and 90% of bulbs were off.
   10% + 90% = 100%

A whole is always 100%.

80 of the 100 sweets are blue.
80% of the sweets are blue.

How many sweets are not blue?
   100% − 80% = 20%

20% are **not** blue.

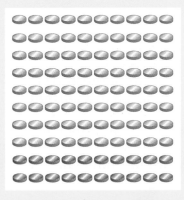

3 There are 100 cats.

a How many cats are black?

b What percentage of the cats are black?

c What percentage of the cats are not black?

4 Carla has 100 pencils.
50 are black. The rest are red.

a What percentage of the pencils are black?

b What percentage of the pencils are red?

5 Mike has 100 bottles of drink.
25 bottles are brown. The rest are green.

   a What percentage of the bottles are brown?

   b What percentage of the bottles are green?

6 Samuel has 100 stamps.
45 are French. The rest are British.

   a What percentage of the stamps are French?

   b What percentage of the stamps are British?

82 out of these 100 children have blue eyes.

This is the same as saying that 82% have blue eyes.

16 out of these 100 children are left-handed.

This is the same as saying that 16% of them are left-handed.

Exercise 9:2

1 Pupils who are right-handed are shaded blue.

   a How many pupils are there altogether?

   b What percentage are right-handed?

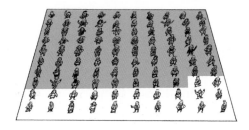

2 Pupils who have school lunch are shaded red.

   a How many pupils are there altogether?

   b What percentage stay for lunch?

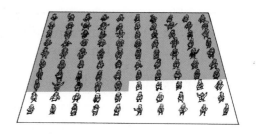

3 Pupils who did not do their homework are shaded green.

   a What percentage did not do their homework?

   b What percentage did do their homework?

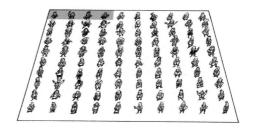

4 Pupils who play in a school sports team are shaded mauve.

   a What percentage play for a school team?

   b What percentage do not play for a school team?

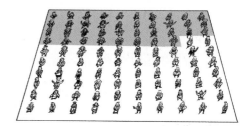

5 Pupils who own a computer are shaded in yellow.

   a What percentage own a computer?

   b What percentage do not own a computer?

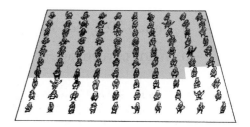

Example   This square is divided into 100 equal pieces. Each piece is 1%.

a Shade 20% red, 30% yellow and 40% blue.

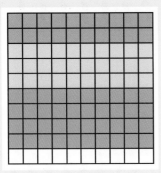

a 20 pieces are shaded red.
30 pieces are shaded yellow.
40 pieces are shaded blue.

b What percentage is unshaded?

b 20% is red, 30% is yellow and 40% is blue.
Altogether 20% + 30% + 40% = 90% is shaded.
100% − 90% = 10% is unshaded.
We can check this by counting the pieces that are not shaded.
There are 10.

Exercise 9:3

 You will need red, blue, green and yellow colouring pencils and Worksheet 1.

1 a Shade 10% green, 40% blue and 20% yellow.

  b What percentage is unshaded?

2 a Shade 30% red, 10% green and 20% blue.

  b What percentage is unshaded?

3 a Shade 20% blue, 20% green and 20% red.

  b What percentage is unshaded?

4 a Shade 30% red, 10% yellow and 60% blue.

  b What percentage is unshaded?

5 a Shade 15% yellow, 25% green and 35% red.

  b What percentage is unshaded?

2 Percentages and decimals

This report uses percentages.
We can also use decimals to show numbers out of a 100
in a different way.
We can work decimals out with a calculator.

Example   Work out 56% as a decimal.

$$56\% = 56 \div 100$$

On a calculator the sum is   5   6   ÷   1   0   0   =

The answer is   0.56

The percentage 56% is 0.56 as a decimal.

Exercise 9:4

1 Use a calculator to change these percentages to decimals.
Write down the calculator sum.

a 35%	**d** 42%	**g** 21%
b 84%	**e** 93%	**h** 68%
c 19%	**f** 77%	

Example Work out 40% as a decimal.

$$40\% = 40 \div 100$$

On a calculator the sum is $\boxed{4}\;\boxed{0}\;\boxed{\div}\;\boxed{1}\;\boxed{0}\;\boxed{0}\;\boxed{=}$

The answer is $\boxed{0.4}$

The percentage 40% is 0.4 as a decimal.

2 Use a calculator to change these percentages to decimals. Write down the calculator sum.

a 70%	**d** 40%	**g** 20%
b 50%	**e** 30%	**h** 10%
c 90%	**f** 60%	

Example **a** Work out 0.64 as a percentage.

a On a calculator the sum is $\boxed{0}\;\boxed{.}\;\boxed{6}\;\boxed{4}\;\boxed{\times}\;\boxed{1}\;\boxed{0}\;\boxed{0}\;\boxed{=}$

The answer is

The decimal 0.64 is 64% as a percentage.

b Work out 0.7 as a percentage.

b On a calculator the sum is $\boxed{0}\;\boxed{.}\;\boxed{7}\;\boxed{\times}\;\boxed{1}\;\boxed{0}\;\boxed{0}\;\boxed{=}$

The answer is

The decimal 0.7 is 70% as a percentage.

3 Use a calculator to change these decimals to percentages. Write down the calculator sum.

a 0.95	**d** 0.47	**g** 0.66
b 0.71	**e** 0.8	**h** 0.5
c 0.2	**f** 0.12	

G 1, 2

3   Fractions and percentages

Fractions are all about dividing a whole into equal pieces.

Half   A half means dividing something into 2 equal pieces.

Exercise 9:5

1   Which of the following cakes have been cut in half?

a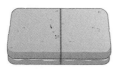

c

b

d

 2   Shade in half of each of these shapes.

a

c

b

d

Sashika has 8 sweets.
She is sharing them equally with her friend Marcus.

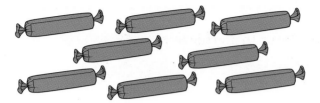

Each of them gets half of the sweets.

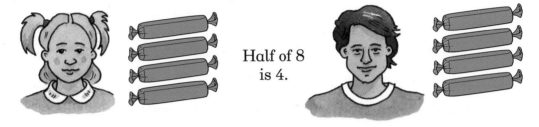

Half of 8
is 4.

| **Finding a half** | By sharing the sweets into 2 equal groups you are **finding a half**. |

3 Jenny has 12 sweets.
She gives half to Helen.
How many sweets do they each have?

4 Simone has 4 biscuits. She gives half to Charlene.
How many biscuits do they each have?

| **Half** | A **half** is also written as $\frac{1}{2}$. This is sharing something into 2 equal pieces. We divide (or share) by 2 to calculate $\frac{1}{2}$. |
| *Example* | What is $\frac{1}{2}$ of 6? $\frac{1}{2}$ of $6 = 6 \div 2 = 3$ |

5 **a** What is $\frac{1}{2}$ of 10?   **d** What is $\frac{1}{2}$ of 20?

   b What is $\frac{1}{2}$ of 14?   **e** What is $\frac{1}{2}$ of 16?

   c What is $\frac{1}{2}$ of 12?   **f** What is $\frac{1}{2}$ of 100?

Example   What is $\frac{1}{2}$ of 56?

$\frac{1}{2}$ of $56 = 56 \div 2$

We can use a calculator to do this sum   5   6   ÷   2   =

The answer is   28.

$\frac{1}{2}$ of $56 = 56 \div 2 = 28$

6 Use a calculator to find the answers.
Write down the calculator sum for each question.

a $\frac{1}{2}$ of 82   **d** $\frac{1}{2}$ of 210

b $\frac{1}{2}$ of 68   **e** $\frac{1}{2}$ of 90

c $\frac{1}{2}$ of 46   **f** $\frac{1}{2}$ of 24

| **Quarter** | A **quarter** means dividing something into 4 equal pieces. |

Exercise 9:6

1 Which of the following cakes have been cut into quarters?

a   **b**   **c**   **d**

W3 **2** Shade in a quarter of each of these shapes.

a   **b**   **c**   **d**

Chris has 12 models.
He is sharing them equally
with his friends Oliver,
Andrew and Ryall.
Each of them gets a quarter
of the models.
A quarter of 12 is 3.

| **Finding a quarter** | By sharing the models into 4 equal groups you are **finding a quarter**. |

3   Alice has 8 sweets.
She shares them equally with her friends Katie, Jack and Heidi.
They have a quarter of the sweets each.
How many sweets does each child have?
(You can use counters to help you.)

4   Elizabeth has 24 biscuits.
She shares them equally with Rebecca, Sue and Steve.
How many biscuits do they have each?

| **Quarter** | A **quarter** is also written as $\frac{1}{4}$. This is sharing something into 4 equal pieces. We divide (or share) by 2 to calculate $\frac{1}{4}$. |
| *Example* | What is $\frac{1}{4}$ of 16? $\frac{1}{4}$ of 16 = 16 ÷ 4 = 4 |

5   **a** What is $\frac{1}{4}$ of 20?

b What is $\frac{1}{2}$ of 40?

Example What is $\frac{1}{4}$ of 72?

$\frac{1}{4}$ of $72 = 72 \div 4$

We can use a calculator to do this sum | 7 | 2 | ÷ | 4 | = |

The answer is | 18. |

$\frac{1}{4}$ of $72 = 72 \div 4 = 18$

6 Use a calculator to find the answers.
Write down the calculator sum for each question.

a What is $\frac{1}{4}$ of 84? **d** What is $\frac{1}{4}$ of 200?

b What is $\frac{1}{4}$ of 68? **e** What is $\frac{1}{4}$ of 44?

c What is $\frac{1}{4}$ of 96? **f** What is $\frac{1}{4}$ of 52?

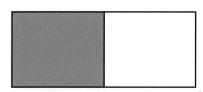

1 piece shaded out of 2 is written $\frac{1}{2}$.

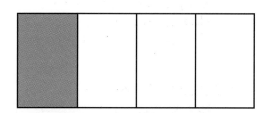

1 piece shaded out of 4 is written $\frac{1}{4}$.

How is 1 piece out of 100 written?

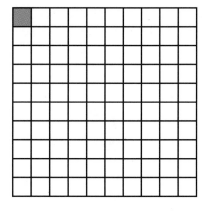

$\dfrac{1}{100}$

This is **one hundredth**.

Example	What is 16% as a fraction?	$16\% = 16 \text{ out of } 100 = \dfrac{16}{100}$

Exercise 9:7

1 Write these percentages as fractions.

a $42\% = \dfrac{?}{100}$ **c** $93\% = \dfrac{?}{100}$ **e** 18%   **g** 10%

b $39\% = \dfrac{?}{100}$ **d** $25\% = \dfrac{?}{100}$ **f** 75%   **h** 80%

Example	What is $\dfrac{45}{100}$ as a percentage?	$\dfrac{45}{100} = 45\%$

2 Write these fractions as percentages.

a $\dfrac{61}{100} = ?\%$ **c** $\dfrac{33}{100}$ **e** $\dfrac{74}{100}$ **g** $\dfrac{89}{100}$

b $\dfrac{96}{100} = ?\%$ **d** $\dfrac{48}{100}$ **f** $\dfrac{52}{100}$ **h** $\dfrac{14}{100}$

Example	**a** What is $\dfrac{40}{100}$ as a percentage?	$\dfrac{40}{100} = 40\%$
	b What is $\dfrac{4}{100}$ as a percentage?	$\dfrac{4}{100} = 4\%$

3 Write these fractions as percentages.

a $\dfrac{60}{100} = ?\%$ **c** $\dfrac{30}{100}$ **e** $\dfrac{7}{100}$ **g** $\dfrac{8}{100}$

b $\dfrac{50}{100} = ?\%$ **d** $\dfrac{10}{100}$ **f** $\dfrac{5}{100}$ **h** $\dfrac{3}{100}$

G 3, 4

4 Percentages, decimals and fractions

They are all the same mark.

Example Shade 43 out of 100 on the square.
Then work out 43 out of 100 as a percentage, a decimal, a fraction.

Percentage	Decimal	Fraction
43%	0.43	$\frac{43}{100}$

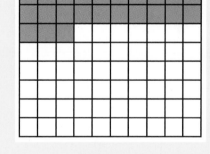

Exercise 9:8

1 For each of the questions shade the square on Worksheet 4 and fill in the table to show the percentage, decimal and fraction.

a 35 out of 100   **d** 15 out of 100   **g** 5 out of 100

b 76 out of 100   **e** 45 out of 100   **h** 25 out of 100

c 99 out of 100   **f** 50 out of 100   **i** 75 out of 100

5   **2**   Fill in the gaps in the table.

	Percentage	Decimal	Fraction
a	23%		
b			$\dfrac{38}{100}$
c			$\dfrac{56}{100}$
d		0.2	
e		0.82	
f			$\dfrac{40}{100}$
g	63%		
h	19%		

G 5, 6, 7

1 **a** How many of the baseball players are wearing red hats?

   b Write this in words out of one hundred.

   c Write this as a percentage.

   d How many baseball players have blue hats?

   e Write this in words out of one hundred.

   f Write this as a percentage.

2 Carla has 100 pencils. 40 are black. The rest are red.

   a What percentage of the pencils are black?

   b What percentage of the pencils are red?

3 Pupils who own a Gameboy are shaded in blue.

   a What percentage of pupils own a Gameboy?

   b What percentage do not own a Gameboy?

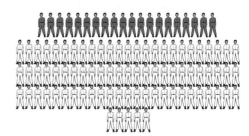

 4 **a** On Worksheet 6 shade 50% green, 10% blue and 10% yellow.

   b What percentage is unshaded?

 5 **a** On Worksheet 6 shade 30% red, 45% green and 15% blue.

   b What percentage is unshaded?

 6 **a** On Worksheet 6 shade 22% blue, 32% green and 41% red.

   b What percentage is unshaded?

7 Use a calculator to change these percentages to decimals. Write down the calculator sum.

   a 24%   **c** 12%   **e** 99%   **g** 28%

   b 65%   **d** 36%   **f** 71%   **h** 66%

8 Use a calculator to change these decimals to percentages.
Write down the calculator sum.

   a 0.22   **c** 0.61   **e** 0.35   **g** 0.8

   b 0.56   **d** 0.99   **f** 0.87   **h** 0.25

9 Use a calculator to find the answers.
Write down the calculator sum for each question.

   a $\frac{1}{2}$ of 34   **c** $\frac{1}{2}$ of 44   **e** $\frac{1}{2}$ of 28   **g** $\frac{1}{2}$ of 12

   b $\frac{1}{2}$ of 60   **d** $\frac{1}{2}$ of 36   **f** $\frac{1}{2}$ of 82   **h** $\frac{1}{2}$ of 58

10 Use a calculator to find the answers.
Write down the calculator sum for each question.

   a $\frac{1}{4}$ of 48   **c** $\frac{1}{4}$ of 92   **e** $\frac{1}{4}$ of 124   **g** $\frac{1}{4}$ of 60

   b $\frac{1}{4}$ of 28   **d** $\frac{1}{4}$ of 88   **f** $\frac{1}{4}$ of 32   **h** $\frac{1}{4}$ of 72

11 Write these percentages as fractions.

   a $32\% = \dfrac{?}{100}$ **b** 60%   **c** 56%   **d** 21%

12 Write these fractions as percentages.

   a $\dfrac{25}{100} = ?\%$ **b** $\dfrac{41}{100}$ **c** $\dfrac{83}{100}$ **d** $\dfrac{62}{100}$

13 Write these fractions as percentages.

   a $\dfrac{20}{100} = ?\%$ **b** $\dfrac{80}{100}$ **c** $\dfrac{9}{100}$ **d** $\dfrac{2}{100}$

W7

14 For each of the questions shade the square on Worksheet 7 and
fill in the table to show the percentage, decimal and fraction.

   a 55 out of 100   **c** 18 out of 100

   b 30 out of 100   **d** 86 out of 100

10 Straight lines

The co-ordinates we use to draw graphs are called Cartesian co-ordinates. They were named after a Frenchman called René Descartes (1596–1650). In 1619 he had a dream in which he realised that all the sciences were connected and that physics could be expressed using the language of geometry. One of Descartes' famous sayings was: '*Cogito ergo sum*' which is Latin for '*Je pense, donc je suis*'.

1 Lines of the grid

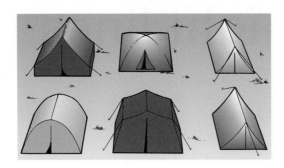

Exercise 10:1

Oliver owns a camp site.
In his office he has
a picture to show him
which pitches are empty.

Oliver can see that
pitch (2, blue) is empty.

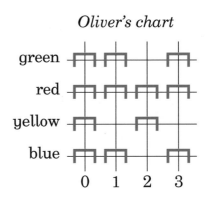

Oliver's chart

1 a Which other 3 pitches on Oliver's campsite are empty?

b Column 0 is full. Which row is full?

James owns a different
camp site.
He has a different chart
to show him which pitches
are empty.
James can see that pitch
(3, 0) is empty.

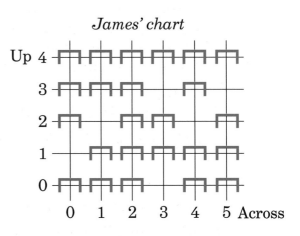

James' chart

2 Which other 5 pitches on James' campsite are empty?

You draw a horizontal line and a vertical line known as **axes**.

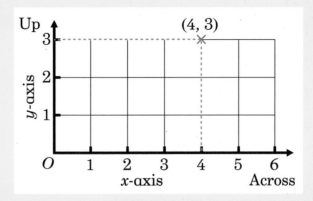

x-axis

The horizontal line (across) is called the **x-axis**.

y-axis

The vertical line (up) is called the **y-axis**.

Co-ordinates

You use two numbers to mark a point.
These numbers are called **co-ordinates**.
Co-ordinates are written like this $(4, 3)$
This means it is across 4 and up 3.
You write the across number first from the x-axis.
You write the up number last from the y-axis.
The x co-ordinate is 4.
The y co-ordinate is 3.

On James' chart the 4th row is full of tents.
The pitches on the 4th row are $(0, 4)$, $(1, 4)$, $(2, 4)$, $(3, 4)$, $(4, 4)$, $(5, 4)$.
All of these pitches have the same second co-ordinate.
The second co-ordinate is the y co-ordinate.

All of these pitches have $y = 4$.
The rule for this line of pitches is $y = 4$.

Look back at the chart for James' camp site.

3   **a**   Which column is full of tents?

     b   Write down the co-ordinates of all the pitches in the full column.

     c   Which co-ordinate is the same for all of these pitches, x or y?

     d   What is the rule for this line of pitches?

The next week James has different campers and a different chart.

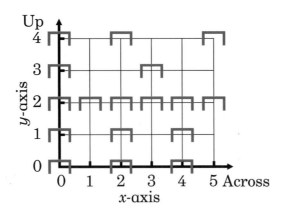

4   **a** Which column is full of tents?

  b Write down the co-ordinates of all the pitches in the full column.

  c Which co-ordinate is the same for all of these pitches?

  d What is the rule for this line of pitches?

5   **a** Which row is full of tents?

  b Write down the co-ordinates of all the pitches in the full row.

  c Which co-ordinate is the same for all of these pitches?

  d What is the rule for this line of pitches?

Exercise 10:2

1   Look at the red line.
    The co-ordinates of the
    point P are $(2, 3)$.

  a Write down the
      co-ordinates of the
      points A, B, C and D.

  b Write down the rule
      for the line.

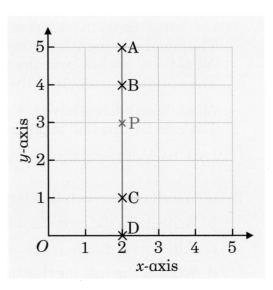

2 Look at the red line.

  a Write down the co-ordinates of the points A, B, C, D and E.

  b Write down the rule for the line.

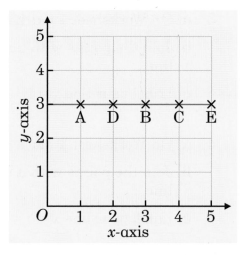

The red line has the rule $x = 2$.
All the points on the line have co-ordinates $(2, ?)$,
e.g. $(2, 0)$, $(2, 4)$ and $(2, 10)$.

$x = 3$ is a vertical line.

The blue line has the rule $x = 7$.
All the points on the line have co-ordinates $(7, ?)$,
e.g. $(7, 1)$, $(7, 4)$ and $(7, 11)$.

$x = 7$ is a vertical line.

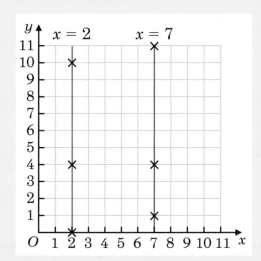

The green line has the rule $y = 5$.
All the points on the line have co-ordinates $(?, 5)$,
e.g. $(3, 5)$, $(4, 5)$ and $(9, 5)$.

$y = 5$ is a horizontal line.

The black line has the rule $y = 8$.
All the points on the line have co-ordinates $(?, 8)$,
e.g. $(2, 8)$, $(7, 8)$ and $(8, 8)$.

$y = 8$ is a horizontal line.

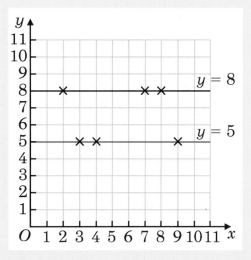

1   **3** **a** On Worksheet 1 mark 4 points that will be on the line $x = 1$

b Join the points with a ruler. They should all be on a straight line.

c Label your line $x = 1$

 1   **4** **a** On Worksheet 1 mark 4 points that will be on the line $x = 6$

b Join the points with a ruler. They should all be on a straight line.

c Label your line $x = 6$

 1   **5** **a** On Worksheet 1 mark 4 points that will be on the line $y = 2$

b Join the points with a ruler. They should all be on a straight line.

c Label your line $y = 2$

 1   **6** **a** On Worksheet 1 mark 4 points that will be on the line $y = 4$

b Join the points with a ruler. They should all be on a straight line.

c Label your line $y = 4$

The green line is $x = 4$

The red line is $y = 3$

The lines cross at the point $(4, 3)$

We say the **point of intersection** is $(4, 3)$

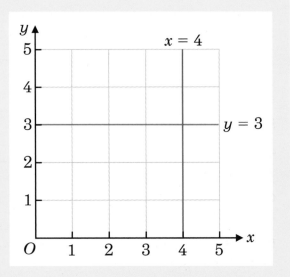

W 2   **7**   **a** On Worksheet 2 draw the line $x = 3$
Label the line with its rule.

     b Draw the line $y = 2$
Label the line with its rule.

     c The lines cross at a point of intersection.
What are the co-ordinates of the point of intersection?

W 2   **8**   **a** On Worksheet 2 draw the line $x = 10$
Label the line with its rule.

     b Draw the line $y = 5$
Label the line with its rule.

     c The lines cross at a point of intersection.
What are the co-ordinates of the point of intersection?

W 2   **9**   **a** On Worksheet 2 draw the line $x = 0$
Label the line with its rule.

     b Draw the line $y = 0$
Label the line with its rule.

     c The lines cross at a point of intersection.
What are the co-ordinates of the point of intersection?

G 1, 2, 3

The line $y = 0$ is also called the x-axis.

The line $x = 0$ is also called the y-axis.

The **point of intersection** of the x-axis and y-axis has co-ordinates $(0, 0)$. It is called the **origin**.

2   Patterns of lines

Matthew and Katy are looking for patterns on a grid.

Matthew has put some counters on points of the grid.
He wants the y co-ordinate to be the same as the x co-ordinate.
So if $x = 1$ then $y = 1$ and the point is $(1, 1)$.

Exercise 10:3

 You will need Worksheet 3. Use Matthew's pattern.

1   a If $x = 2$, what is y?
    b What are the co-ordinates of this point?
    c Mark this point on your grid.

2   a If $x = 5$, what is y?
    b What are the co-ordinates of this point?
    c Mark this point on your grid.

3   a If $x = 9$, what is y?
    b What are the co-ordinates of this point?
    c Mark this point on your grid.

4   a If $x = 12$, what is y?
    b What are the co-ordinates of this point?
    c Mark this point on your grid.

5   a Mark 4 more points on your grid which are true for the
       rule $y = x$.
    b Join the points with a straight line.
    c Label the line $y = x$.

Patterns from co-ordinates

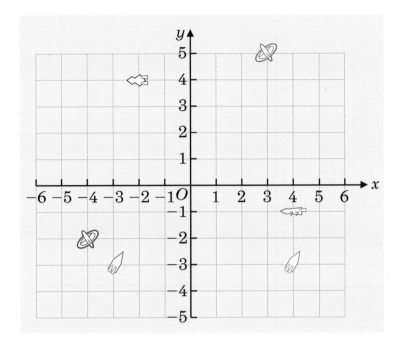

The x-axis and y-axis can be extended into negative numbers.
The point of intersection of the axes is at $(0,0)$.

The x co-ordinate (across) still always comes first then the y co-ordinate (up or down).

| Red space station | $(3,5)$ | Blue rocket | $(-3,-3)$ |
| Transporter | $(-2,4)$ | Shuttle | $(4,-1)$ |

Exercise 10:4

1 What are the co-ordinates of the red rocket?

2 What are the co-ordinates of the blue space station?

 3 **a** On Worksheet 4 fill in the missing numbers on the axes.

b Draw these symbols at the co-ordinates given.

Red transporter	at $(5,-2)$	Blue shuttle	at $(8,7)$
Blue rocket	at $(-4,5)$	Red space station	at $(-6,-3)$
Red shuttle	at $(0,5)$	Red rocket	at $(-5,4)$
Blue space station	at $(-5,-2)$	Blue transporter	at $(7,-6)$

181

W 5   **4**   You need a grid like this:

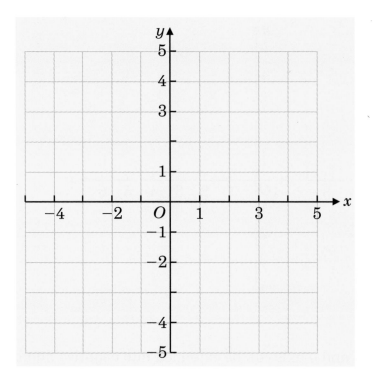

Fill in the missing numbers on the axes.

W 5   **5**   Plot these co-ordinates on the same grid.

a $(1, 1), (3, 1), (3, 3), (1, 3)$
Join the points in order, ending back at the first point.
What shape is this?

b $(-1, 4), (-4, 1), (-1, -1)$
Join the points in order, ending back at the first point.
What shape is this?

c $(-1, -1), (-1, -2), (-4, -2), (-4, -1)$
Join the points in order, ending back at the first point.
What shape is this?

d $(2, -1), (3, -1), (4, -2), (3, -3), (2, -3), (1, -2)$
Join the points in order, ending back at the first point.
What shape is this?

5   **6**   You need a grid like this:

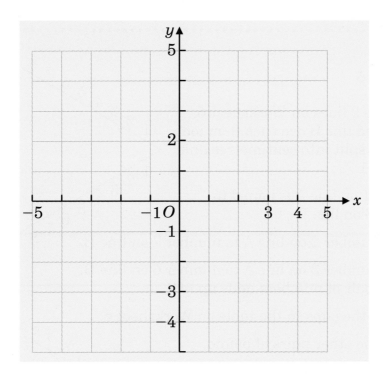

Fill in the missing numbers on the axes.

 5   **7**   Plot these points.

$(0, 5)$, $(1, 2)$, $(3, 3)$, $(2, 1)$, $(5, 0)$, $(2, -1)$, $(3, -3)$, $(1, -2)$, $(0, -5)$, $(-1, -2)$, $(-3, -3)$, $(-2, -1)$, $(-5, 0)$, $(-2, 1)$, $(-3, 3)$, $(-1, 2)$

Join the points with a ruler as you go, ending back at the first point.

 5   **8**   Design a picture of your own.

Write down the co-ordinates of your points so that one of your friends can follow them to draw your picture.

 6

3 Curves from straight lines

Exercise 10:5

W 6 **1** There are 2 lines on Worksheet 6.
Line A and line B are each 8 cm long.
They are split into centimetres and
numbered.

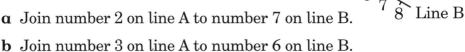

Number 1 on line A is joined to
number 8 on line B.

  a Join number 2 on line A to number 7 on line B.

  b Join number 3 on line A to number 6 on line B.
  Each pair of numbers adds up to 9.

  c Fill in the gaps in the table on Worksheet 6.

  d Join the other pairs of points.

You should get a pattern like this.

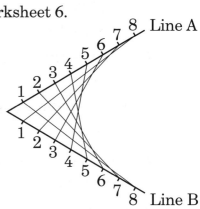

W 6 **2** On Worksheet 6 there are another 2 lines.
Line C and line D are each 8 cm long.
They are split into half centimetres and numbered.

Number 1 on line C is joined to number 16 on line D.

  a Join number 2 on line C to number 15 on line D.

  b Join number 3 on line C to number 14 on line D.
  Each pair of numbers adds up to 17.

  c Fill in the gaps in the table on Worksheet 6.

  d Join the other pairs of points.

You should get a better curve when the marked points are
closer together like this.

W 7 **3** On Worksheet 7 there is a diagram like this:

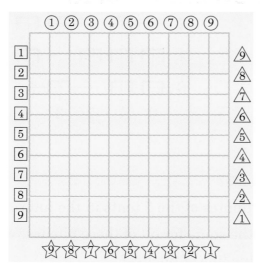

a Join the circle and triangle numbers so that ① joins ⑨ , ② joins ⑧ , and so on.

Each pair of numbers adds up to 10.

b Join the circle and square numbers ① to ⑨ , ② to ⑧ , and so on.

c Join the triangle and star numbers ⑨ to ⑦ , ⑧ to ⑦ , and so on.

d Join the square and the star numbers ① to ⑨ , ② to ⑧ , and so on.

You should get a pattern like this.

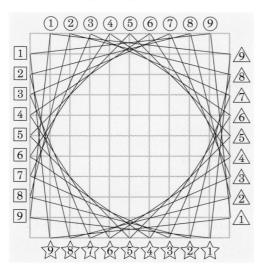

1 What are the co-ordinates of the five empty pitches on this campsite?

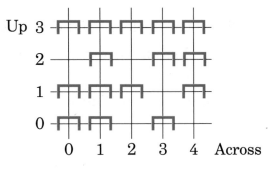

2 Look at the chart above.

a Which row is full of tents?

b Write down the co-ordinates of the 5 tents in the full row.

c Which co-ordinate is the same for all of these pitches, x or y?

d What is the rule for this line of pitches?

3 Look at the chart above.

a Which column is full of tents?

b Write down the co-ordinates of the 4 tents in the full column.

c Which co-ordinate is the same for all of these pitches, x or y?

d What is the rule for this line of pitches?

4 Look at the red line.

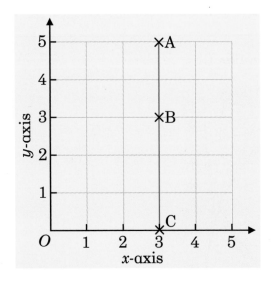

a Write down the co-ordinates of the points A, B and C.

b Write down the rule for the line.

5 **a** On Worksheet 8 mark 4 points that will be on the line $y = 3$.

    b Join the points with a ruler. They should all be on a straight line.

    c Label your line $y = 3$.

6 **a** On Worksheet 8 mark 4 points that will be on the line $x = 4$.

    b Join the points with a ruler. They should all be on a straight line.

    c Label your line $x = 4$.

7 **a** On Worksheet 8 draw the line $x = 2$.
Label the line with its rule.

    b Draw the line $y = 4$.
Label the line with its rule.

    c The lines cross at a point of intersection.
What are the co-ordinates of the point of intersection?

8 What is the special name of the point with co-ordinates $(0,0)$?

9 On Worksheet 8 you are going to draw 2 different shapes on the same grid.

    a Plot the co-ordinates

        $(-2, -2), (-2, 3), (0, 5), (2, 5), (4, 3), (4, -2)$

    Join the points in order, ending back at the first point.

    b Plot the co-ordinates

        $(1, -2), (1, 1), (2, 1), (2, -2)$

    Join the points in order.

11 Ratio

Most maps of the UK are produced from the Ordnance Survey. The Board of Ordnance used to be in charge of defending Britain. (Ordnance means military supplies.) They wanted good maps for soldiers to use so they began the Ordnance Survey.

The Ordnance Survey put 'bench marks' in places like the stone of bridges or on the tops of hills. They use these points to measure from.

A bench mark

A large-scale Ordnance Survey map

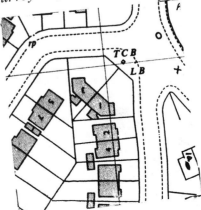

The Ordnance Survey brings maps up to date from time to time. They mark new buildings and roads.

They produce large-scale maps and smaller-scale maps.

1   The metric system

Jane and Andy have broken a window. Their father is measuring the window for glass. He is measuring in millimetres.

◀◀**REPLAY**▶

Exercise 11:1

1 Make a millimetre/centimetre ruler.

2 Use your ruler to measure these items in your classroom.
Write the measurements in your book.
Give your answers in centimetres.

   a The length of your pen.   **c** The width of your desk.

   b The thickness of this book.   **d** The length of your foot.

3 **a** Which is the shortest?

   b Which is the longest?

4 Measure some more items in your classroom.
Write down the name and the measurement for each.

There are 10 millimetres in 1 centimetre

   $10\,mm = 1\,cm$

Roy uses his ruler to change centimetres to millimetres.

   1 centimetre = 10 millimetres
   2 centimetres = 20 millimetres
   3 centimetres = 30 millimetres

5 You can use your ruler to help you with these questions. Match the centimetres with the millimetres. Write a sentence for each one: *'9 centimetres is 90 millimetres.'*

Centimetres	Millimetres
9	80
4	90
10	60
8	40
6	100

6 Can you write a rule for changing centimetres to millimetres?

Marie uses her ruler to change millimetres to centimetres.

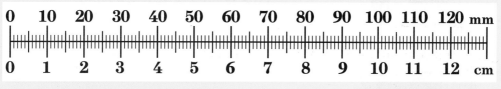

20 millimetres = 2 centimetres
30 millimetres = 3 centimetres
40 millimetres = 4 centimetres

7 You can use your ruler to help you with these questions. Match the millimetres with the centimetres. Write a sentence for each one: *'20 millimetres is 2 centimetres.'*

Millimetres	Centimetres
20	7
70	3
50	2
30	11
110	5

8 Can you write down a rule for changing millimetres to centimetres?

 G 1, 2

Exercise 11:2

W 2 **1** Make a centimetre/metre ruler.

2 Use your ruler to measure these items in your classroom.
Write the measurements in your book.
Give your answers in metres and centimetres.

  a The height of your desk.   **c** The height of the window.

  b The width of the door.   **d** The length of your foot.

3 a Which is the shortest?

   b Which is the longest?

4 Measure some more items in your classroom.
Write down the name and the measurement for each.

There are 100 centimetres in 1 metre.

   $100\,cm = 1\,m$

This is part of Karla's ruler.

15 cm   20 cm   25 cm   30 cm   35 cm

Karla uses her rule to change metres to centimetres.

   1 metre = 100 centimetres
   2 metres = 200 centimetres
   3 metres = 300 centimetres

---

5 You can use your ruler or a metre stick to help you with
these questions.
Match the metres with the centimetres.
Write a sentence for each one:
'4 metres is 400 centimetres.'

Metres	Centimetres
4	800
7	700
10	1000
6	400
8	600

6 Can you write a rule for changing metres to centimetres?

Alice uses her ruler to change centimetres to metres.

400 centimetres = 4 metres
500 centimetres = 5 metres
900 centimetres = 9 metres

7 You can use your ruler to help you with these questions.
Match the centimetres with the metres.
Write a sentence for each one:
'100 centimetres is 1 metre.'

Centimetres	Metres
100	8
300	11
1100	2
200	3
800	1

8 Can you write down a rule for changing centimetres to metres?

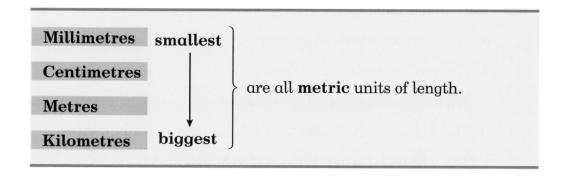

Exercise 11:3

1 Write these measurements in order, smallest first.
You can use your rulers to help you.

   a 31 millimetres   20 millimetres   80 millimetres   5 millimetres

   b 17 centimetres   8 centimetres   120 centimetres   52 centimetres

   c 400 metres   240 metres   75 metres   800 metres

   d 130 kilometres   12 kilometres   85 kilometres   65 kilometres

2 Write these measurements in order, smallest first.

   a 5 kilometres   5 millimetres   5 metres   5 centimetres

   b 25 metres   25 centimetres   25 kilometres   25 millimetres

   c 11 millimetres   11 kilometres   11 centimetres   11 metres

Mahesh is measuring his tie.
He has used the wrong metric units.
He has written:

My tie measures 22 kilometres.

He should have written:

My tie measures 22 centimetres.

3 Write each sentence with the correct metric unit.
You can use your rulers to help you.

   a The desk measures 55 metres.

   b The book measures 26 kilometres.

   c My finger measures 75 centimetres.

   d The distance from home to school measures 3 millimetres.

   e The width of my pencil measures 8 metres.

Weighing

Things are **weighed** using scales.
There are different types of scales.

These apples weigh 1 kg 350 grams.
This is also written as 1.350 kg.

This is how they look on three different types of scales:

Exercise 11:4

1 How much do these tomatoes weigh?

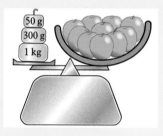

2 How much does this melon weigh?

3 How much do these bananas weigh?

4 How much do these mangoes weigh?

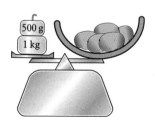

5 What is the weight of these mushrooms?

6 What is the weight of these carrots?

7 Weigh each of these items from your classroom.
Write down the weight in kilograms and grams.

  a This textbook.

  b A pencil case.

  c A calculator.

  d 10 exercise books.

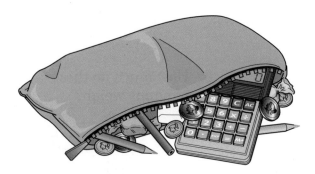

8 Weigh some more items from your classroom.
Draw a table like this in your book:

item	weight

Write down the name and weight of each item in the table.

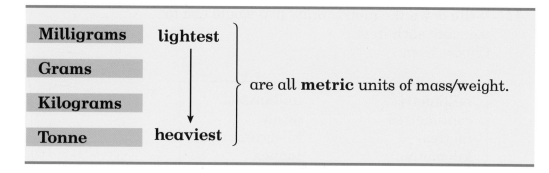

Milligrams	lightest	
Grams		
Kilograms		are all **metric** units of mass/weight.
Tonne	heaviest	

9   Write these weights in order, lightest first.
You can use scales to help you.

a 20 kilograms   20 milligrams   20 tonnes   20 grams

b 750 milligrams   750 tonnes   750 grams   750 kilograms

c 45 grams   45 kilograms   45 milligrams   45 tonnes

G 5, 6   **d** 45 milligrams   6 tonnes   700 grams   30 kilograms

Tracey is weighing flour.
She has used the wrong
metric units.
She has written:

The flour weighs 500 tonnes.

She should have written:

The flour weighs 500 grams.

10   Write each sentence with the correct metric unit.
You can use scales to help you.

a The lorry weighs 3 milligrams.

b The sugar weighs 2.5 tonnes.

c The parcel weighs 650 kilograms.

d The man weighs 90 grams.

11 Write down the metric units you would use to measure each item.
Choose from:

millimetres	milligrams
centimetres	grams
metres	kilograms
kilometres	tonnes

a The height of a lighthouse.

b The weight of an elephant.

c The width of bus.

d The length of piece of string.

e The weight of a drawing pin.

f The weight of a watch.

g The distance from London to Paris.

2 Changing sizes

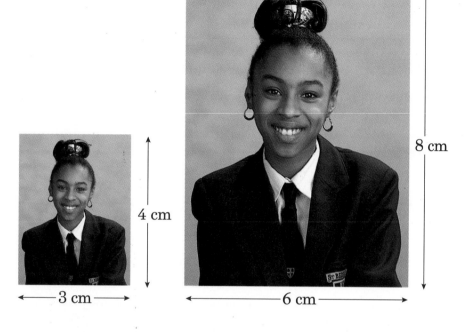

4 cm

8 cm

← 3 cm →

← 6 cm →

Year 8 have had their photographs taken.

This is Sonya's picture.

The **width** of the large photograph is **twice as long** as the small photograph.
The **length** of the large photograph is **twice as long** as the small photograph.

Exercise 11:5

1 **a** Measure this square.
Copy it into your book.

b Draw a new square with sides **twice** as long.

c Draw another new square with sides **half** as long.

2 a Measure this rectangle.
Copy it into your book.

b Draw a new rectangle with sides **twice** as long.

c Draw another new rectangle with sides **three times** as long.

| Ratio | **Ratio** is a way of comparing quantities. |

This pattern is made with cubes.

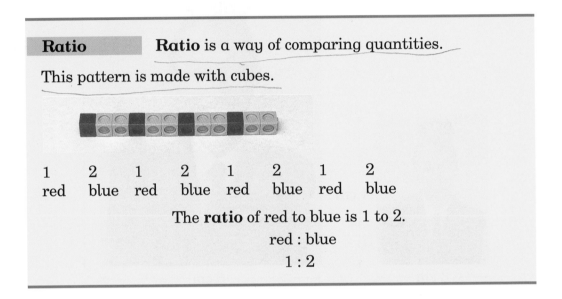

1	2	1	2	1	2	1	2
red	blue	red	blue	red	blue	red	blue

The **ratio** of red to blue is 1 to 2.

red : blue

1 : 2

3

a Make this cube pattern.

b Write down the ratio of red : blue.

4

a Make this cube pattern.

b Write down the ratio of black : yellow.

5

a Make this cube pattern

b Write down the ratio of green : red.

6 Make a cube pattern with ratio 2:1. Draw it in your book.

7 Make a cube pattern with ratio 1:5. Draw it in your book.

8 Make a cube pattern with ratio 3:1. Draw it in your book.

3 Recipes

Robert is cooking some fruit buns.

The recipe is for 20 buns but Robert only wants to make 10.

He needs to change the amounts in the recipe.

He halves or ÷2

Changing recipes

This recipe is for **2** people.

> **Mexican Re-fried Beans**
> **20** ml oil
> **1** small onion
> **1** garlic clove
> **1** green chilli
> **200** grams cooked red beans

Here it is for **4** people.

> **Mexican Re-fried Beans**
> **40** ml oil
> **2** small onions
> **2** garlic cloves
> **1** green chilli
> **400** grams cooked red beans

The number of people has **doubled** so the quantities **double** or ×2.

Exercise 11:6

 1 Recipe for 4 people.

> **Chicken mayonnaise**
> 4 chicken breasts
> 2 celery sticks
> 200 ml mayonnaise
> 100 ml chicken stock

Write the recipe for 8 people.

2 Recipe for 8 people.

> **Homemade muesli**
> 200 g oats
> 100 g raisins
> 100 g chopped nuts and seeds

Write this recipe for 4 people.

 3 Recipe for 10 buns.

> 150 g self-raising flour
> 100 g soft margarine
> 100 g castor sugar
> 2 large eggs

Write this recipe for 20 buns.

 4 Recipe for 24 chapattis

> 450 g wholemeal flour
> 2 teaspoons salt
> $\frac{1}{2}$ pint water

Write this recipe for 12 chapattis.

 5 Recipe for 6 people.

> **Tomato soup**
> 175 ml olive oil
> 4 garlic cloves
> 4 kg ripe tomatoes
> 1 bunch of fresh basil

Write this recipe for 24 people.

4 Maps and scales

Donna is planning
a kitchen.

◀◀ REPLAY ▶

| Scale | The **scale** helps you calculate the real distances from the plan. |

The scale is 1 centimetre to 1 metre

Plan

Kitchen

1 cm

1 metre

The scale is 1 centimetre to 1 kilometre

Map

Road

1 cm

100 m

Use string to find the distance
on the map.

Exercise 11:7

For each question find the distance on the map with string.

Measure the string along a ruler.

Use the scale to find the real distance, for example, 3 cm represents 3 km.

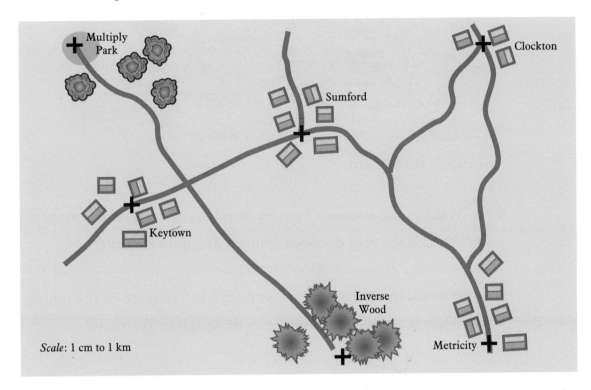

1   a   What is the distance from Keytown to Sumford on the map?

    b   What is the real distance from Keytown to Sumford?

2   a   What is the shortest distance from Clockton to Metricity on the map?

    b   What is the real distance from Clockton to Metricity?

3   a   What is the distance from the centre of Inverse Wood to the centre of Multiply Park on the map?

    b   What is the real distance from the centre of Inverse Wood to the centre of Multiply Park?

This map shows some places in North Wales.

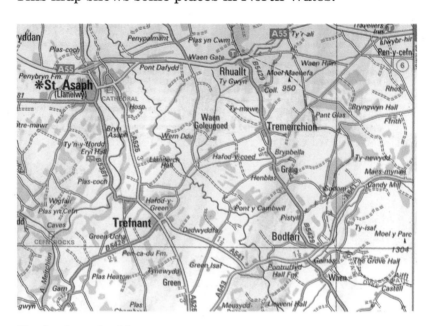

Scale: 1 cm to 1 km

4 a What is the distance from St Asaph to Rhuallt on the map?

    b What is the real distance from St Asaph to Rhuallt?

5 a What is the distance from St Asaph to Trefnant on the map?

    b What is the real distance from St Asaph to Trefnant?

6 a What is the distance from Trefnant to Tremeirchion on the map?

    b What is the real distance from Trefnant to Tremeirchion?

7 a What is the distance from Trefnant to Bodfari on the map?

    b What is the real distance from Trefnant to Bodfari?

8 Find a map with your school and your house on it.

    a What is the distance from your house to your school on the map?

    b Use the scale on the map to find the real distance from your house to your school.

1 How many millimetres are there in a centimetre?

2 How many centimetres are there in a metre?

3 Write these measurements in order, smallest first.

    a 21 millimetres   6 millimetres   10 millimetres   35 millimetres

    b 48 centimetres   76 centimetres   3 centimetres   18 centimetres

    c 7 metres   7 kilometres   7 millimetres   7 centimetres

    d 18 kilometres   18 centimetres   18 millimetres   18 metres

4 The sentences below have been written with the wrong units.
Write the sentences with the correct unit.

    a The door measures 2 centimetres.

    b The pencil measures 15 millimetres.

    c The distance from Cheltenham to Gloucester is 16 metres.

    d The arrow flew 100 kilometres.

5 Write these weights in order, smallest first.

    a 3 grams   3 tonnes   3 milligrams   3 kilograms

    b 56 kilograms   56 milligrams   56 tonnes   56 grams

    c 27 tonnes   34 kilograms   8 grams   91 milligrams

    d 41 milligrams   45 grams   47 tonnes   47 kilograms

6 Write down the metric units you would use to measure the following.

    a The length of a tennis court.

    b The weight of a sack of potatoes.

    c The length of a necklace.

    d The weight of butter.

7 **a** Measure this square.
Copy it into your book.

    b Draw a new square with sides
three times as long.

8

a Make this pattern.

b Write down the ratio of red:blue.

9

a Make this pattern.

b Write down the ratio of red:blue.

10

a Make this pattern.

b Write down the ratio of red:blue.

11   Recipe for 10 buns

> 150 g self-raising flour
> 100 g soft margarine
> 100 g castor sugar
> 2 large eggs

Write this recipe for 5 buns.

12   Recipe for Mexican Re-fried Beans for 4 people.

> 40 ml oil
> 2 small garlic cloves
> 1 green chilli
> 400 g cooked beans

Write this recipe for 8 people.

13   **a** What is the distance from Sanford to Earthy on the map?

b What is the real distance between Sanford and Earthy?

c What is the distance from Cooketon to Earthy on the map?

d What is the real distance from Cooketon to Earthy?

e What is the distance from Kerrby to Harris on the map?

f What is the real distance from Kerrby to Harris?

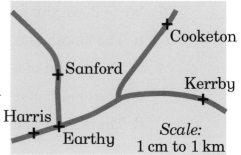

12 Area: covering the ground

QUESTIONS

The surface area of a human lung is approximately the same as the area of a tennis court.

CORE

1   Perimeter and area

◀◀REPLAY▶

This is a picture of York.

It shows the old perimeter wall.

This goes all the way round the outside of the old part of the city.

Perimeter	The total distance around the outside of a shape is its **perimeter**.

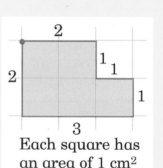

Each square has an area of 1 cm²

The red line is the perimeter of this shape. The measurements are in centimetres.

Start at the red dot.

The perimeter is

$2 + 1 + 1 + 1 + 3 + 2 = 10$ cm

Area	The amount of space inside the shape is called its **area**.

The area of this shape is shaded green.
We use squares to measure area.
There are 5 squares inside this shape.
The area of the shape is 5 square centimetres.
We can write the area of this shape as 5 cm².

Exercise 12 : 1

 1 Copy these shapes on to 1 cm squared paper.
Fill in the gaps.

1

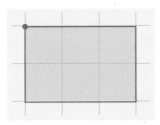

perimeter = …… cm
area = …… cm²

4

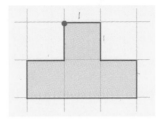

perimeter = …… cm
area = …… cm²

 1 **2**

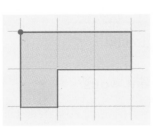

perimeter = …… cm
area = …… cm²

5

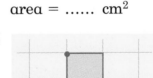

perimeter = …… cm
area = …… cm²

 1 **3**

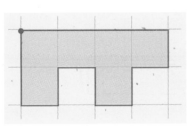

perimeter = …… cm
area = …… cm²

6

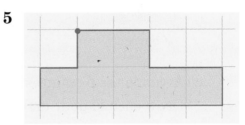

perimeter = …… cm
area = …… cm²

 2 **7** You need some centimetre squared paper.

a Cut out 6 centimetre squares.

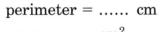

b Put these 6 squares together to make a bigger shape.
For example,

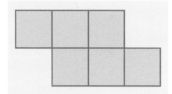

Whole squares must touch – see diagrams below.

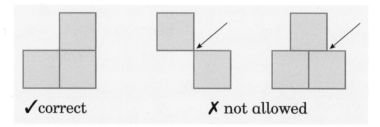

✓ correct   ✗ not allowed

c Arrange the 6 squares in five different ways.
Draw each of your arrangements.

d Work out the perimeter for each shape.
Write the perimeter underneath.

Example

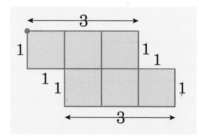

Perimeter $= 3 + 1 + 1 + 1 + 3 + 1 + 1 + 1 = 12$ cm

Rajit wants to find out how many
different rectangles there are that
have a **perimeter** of 16 cm.

He uses string 16 cm long and
squared paper.

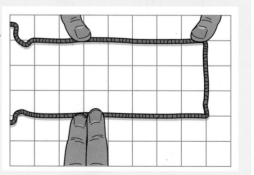

These are the rectangles he found.

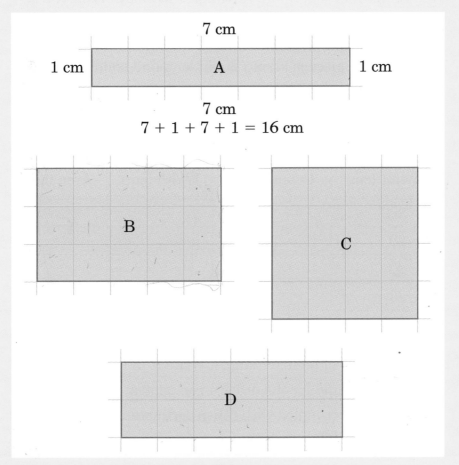

7 cm

1 cm   A   1 cm

7 cm

$7 + 1 + 7 + 1 = 16$ cm

Rajit found four rectangles with a perimeter of 16 cm.
Rajit put his results in a table.

Exercise 12:2

 1 Copy and complete Rajit's table.

Rectangle	Perimeter (cm)	Length (cm)	Width (cm)	Area (cm²)
A	16	7	1	7
B		5		
C	16		4	16
D		6	2	

2 Using Rajit's method, find 5 rectangles with a **perimeter** of 20 cm.

You can work with a partner.

You will need a piece of string 20 cm long and squared paper.

a Use your string to find a rectangle.

b Draw the rectangle.

c Write the length and width of the rectangle in a table.

Perimeter (cm)	Length (cm)	Width (cm)	Area (cm²)
20			
20			
20			
20			
20			

d Find the area of your rectangle. Write it in the table.

e Now do the same for the other 4 rectangles.

f Investigate rectangles with other perimeters using different lengths of string.

Next Rajit looked at rectangles that had the same **area**.
He looked at different rectangles with an area of 20 cm².

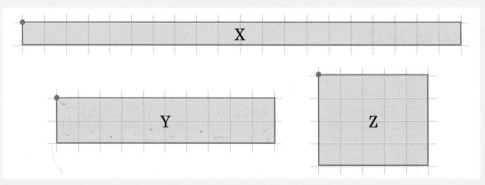

He found three rectangles with an area of 20 cm².
Rajit put his results in a table.

3 Copy and complete Rajit's table.

Rectangle	Length (cm)	Width (cm)	Area (cm²)	Perimeter (cm)
X	20	1	20	42
Y	10			
Z		4	20	

 4 How many rectangles can you find that have an area of $12\,\text{cm}^2$?

    a Draw and label the rectangles on squared paper.

    b Write your results in a table.

Length (cm)	Width (cm)	Area (cm²)	Perimeter (cm)
		12	

    c Do rectangles with the same area have the same perimeter?

    d Rajit found a rule connecting the length and width with the area. If you can see the rule, write it down.

◀◀**REPLAY**▶

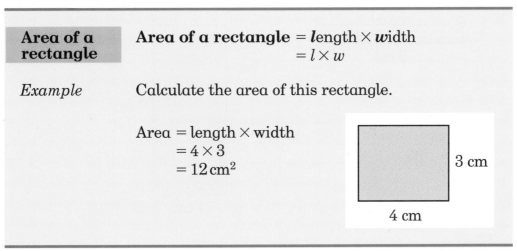

Area of a rectangle

Area of a rectangle = $l$ength × $w$idth
$$= l \times w$$

Example   Calculate the area of this rectangle.

Area = length × width
    = 4 × 3
    = $12\,\text{cm}^2$

3 cm

4 cm

Exercise 12:3

Find the area of these rectangles using the rule.
Write down your working.

1

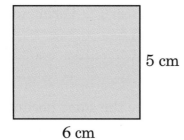

2 cm

5 cm

$A = l \times w$
$\quad = 5 \times 2$
$\quad = 10\,\text{cm}^2$

4

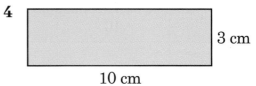

3 cm

10 cm

2

5 cm

6 cm

5

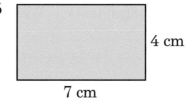

4 cm

7 cm

3

5 cm

8 cm

6

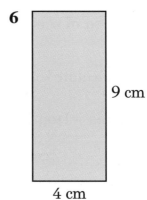

9 cm

4 cm

Alison wants to move
her bedroom furniture.
She needs an empty
space to sort out papers
and she likes to dance
to music.

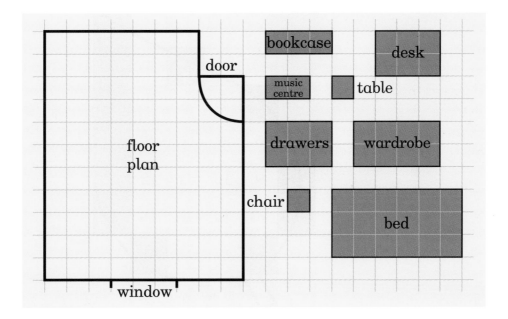

Exercise 12:4

1 **a** Cut out the floor plan and furniture.

   b Arrange the furniture to give Alison as large a space as possible.

   c Stick your plan into your exercise book.

   d On the empty floor space draw the largest rectangle you can fit in.

   e Write down the length and width measurement of your rectangle on the plan.

   f Compare the area of the empty space you arranged with that of other members of your group. Who has the largest?

◄◄ **REPLAY** ▶

The area of some shapes cannot be found exactly.

Example   Estimate the area of this leaf.

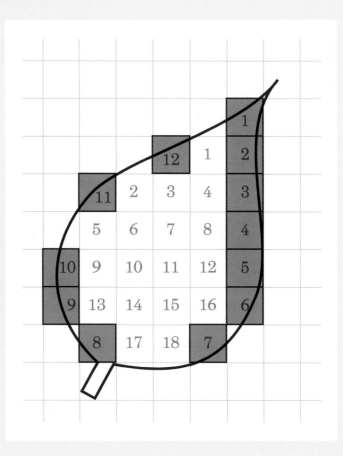

Count whole squares first.
There are **18** whole squares.

Now count squares which lie more than half inside the outline.
There are **12** of these.

An estimate of the area of the leaf is:

18 + **12** = 30 squares.

Exercise 12:5

Estimate the areas of these shapes.
Follow the example.

W 2

1

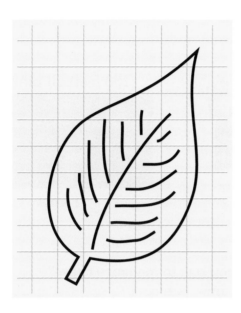

3

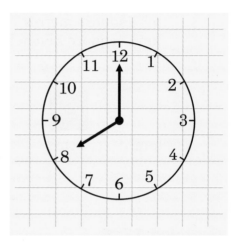

2

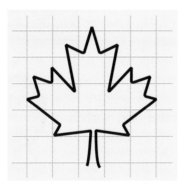

4

Units of area

The area of a shape tells you how much space it covers.

Areas can be measured in
mm² – square millimetres
cm² – square centimetres
m² – square metres
km² – square kilometres.

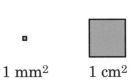

1 mm²   1 cm²

1 m²

200 football pitches

1 km²

Exercise 12:6

1 Which units of area would you use to measure these?
Choose from   mm²,   cm²,   m²,   km².

a Tennis court

d Cornwall

b Postage stamp

e Hand of a watch

c CD case

f Playground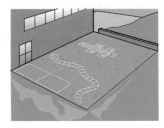

2 List the items above in order of size.
Begin with the one that covers the smallest surface area.

2   Compound shapes

Most rooms are rectangles.

Some rooms are two rectangles put together to make an L shape or a T shape.

Example   Find the area of this L shape.

The shape is made of two rectangles A and B.
The dashed line shows the join.

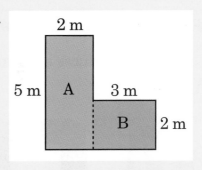

Area of room = area of A + area of B

Area of A = 5×2 = $10\,m^2$

Area of B = 3×2 = $6\,m^2$

Total area = $10 + 6 = 16\,m^2$

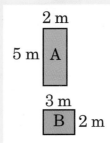

Exercise 12:7

 6

1 Two rectangles have been joined to make this shape.
Copy and complete.

Area of C   = ... × ... = ...m^2

Area of D   = ... × ... = ...m^2

Total area   = ... + ... = ...m^2

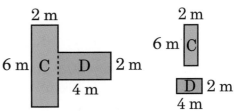

6

2 Find the area of these shapes. Write down all your working.

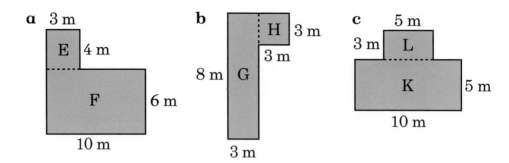

a 3 m
E 4 m
F 6 m
10 m

b
H 3 m
3 m
8 m G
3 m

c 5 m
3 m L
K 5 m
10 m

 3

Finding areas of borders

Some surfaces have spaces inside them.

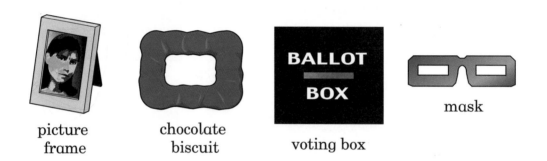

picture
frame

chocolate
biscuit

voting box

mask

Example   This shape has the middle cut out.
Find the area of the piece that is left.

Area of whole $= 10 \times 5$
$= 50 \, \text{cm}^2$

Area of piece cut out $= 5 \times 2$
$= 10 \, \text{cm}^2$

Area of piece left $= 50 - 10$
$= 40 \, \text{cm}^2$

5 cm
2 cm
5 cm
10 cm

Exercise 12:8

Each of these shapes has a piece cut out.
Find the area of the piece that is left.
All measurements are in centimetres.

W4   **1** Copy and fill in:

Area of whole = ... × ...
$$= ... \text{ cm}^2$$

Area of piece cut out = ... × ...
$$= ... \text{ cm}^2$$

Area of piece left = ... − ...
$$= ... \text{ cm}^2$$

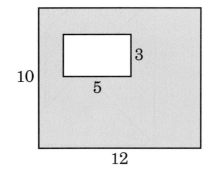

2

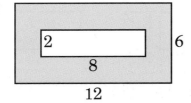

3

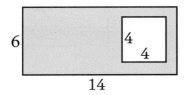

4 **a** Measure the lines w and x.

b Work out the total area.

c Measure the lines y and z.

d Work out the inside area.

e Find the area of the border.

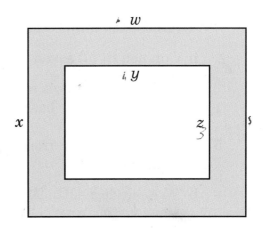

Tangrams

Exercise 12:9

1 Which of these shapes do you think covers the biggest surface area?

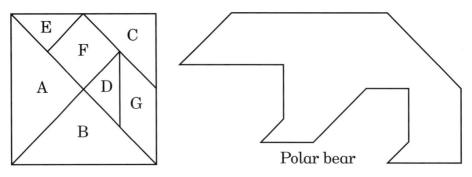

Polar bear

Using the pieces from the square you can make different shapes.

 2

Parallelogram   *Rectangle*

D, E and F will make
both of these shapes.

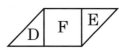

a Make the rectangle.
b Draw and label the rectangle showing the three different pieces.

 3

Square   *Parallelogram*

The square and parallelogram
can be made using 2 triangles.

a Make the shapes.
b Write down which triangles you have used.

4 **a** Use all seven pieces to form the polar bear shape.
(Look back at question 1. Do you still agree with your answer?)

b Can you fit all seven pieces inside the rectangle?

c Use all seven pieces to make your own shape or pattern.
Stick it into your book.

5 **a** Cut out Square 2 from Worksheet 5 and stick it next to
your shape.

b Write underneath, 'My shape and the square cover the
same surface area.'

3 Areas of triangles

The sail of this boat is a triangle.

The makers need to work out the area of this triangle to know how much material to buy.

Exercise 12:10

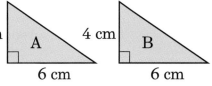

1 a Cut out triangles A and B.
   b Use A and B to make a rectangle.
   c What is the length of the rectangle?
   d What is the width of the rectangle?
   e What is the area of the rectangle?
   f What is the area of triangle A only?

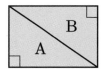

Here is a triangle.
We use **base** and **height**
instead of length and
width.

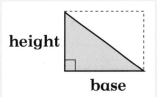

Area of a triangle

$$\text{Area of a triangle} = \frac{\text{area of rectangle}}{2}$$

$$= \frac{\text{base} \times \text{height}}{2}$$

Example   Find the area of this triangle.

$$\text{Area of triangle} = \frac{\text{base} \times \text{height}}{2}$$

$$= \frac{10 \times 8}{2} = \frac{80}{2}$$

$$= 40 \, \text{cm}^2$$

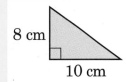

2 Copy and complete.

Area of triangle $= \dfrac{\text{base} \times \text{height}}{2}$

$= \dfrac{10 \times 6}{2}$

$= \dfrac{\ldots}{2}$

$= \ldots \ \text{cm}^2$

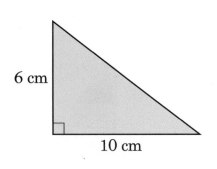

6 cm

10 cm

H 7 Set out the areas of the these triangles in the same way.

3

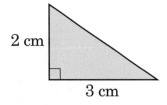

2 cm

3 cm

6

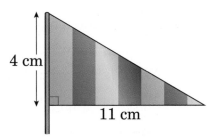

4 cm

11 cm

4

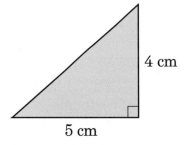

4 cm

5 cm

7

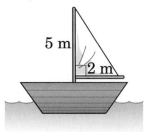

5 m

2 m

5

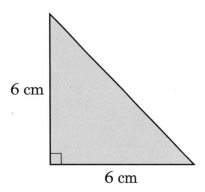

6 cm

6 cm

8

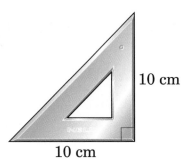

10 cm

10 cm

G 1, 2, 3

226

1 These shapes are drawn on 1 cm squared paper.

a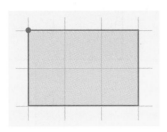

b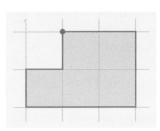

Write down:

i the area of each shape in cm^2

ii the perimeter of each shape in cm.

2 Which units would you use to measure the area of each of these items.
Choose from mm^2, cm^2, m^2, km^2.

a

b

3 Find the area and perimeter of these shapes.
Write down all your working.

a length 4 m

width 3 m

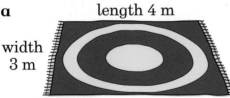

b 10 cm

5 cm

4 Find the area and perimeter of these shapes.

a 3 cm

3 cm

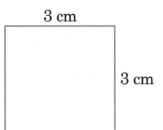

b 6 cm

2 cm

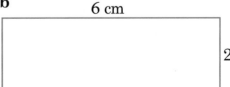

W 8 **5** Work out the area of this shape.
Set your working out as:

Area of C $= \dots \times \dots = \dots$ cm^2

Area of D $= \dots \times \dots = \dots$ cm^2

Total area $= \dots + \dots = \dots$ cm^2

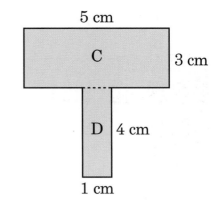

5 cm

C

3 cm

D 4 cm

1 cm

W 8 **6** Work out the area of the
path around the pond.

Set your working out as shown:

Area of whole picture $= \dots \times \dots$

$= \dots$ m^2

Area of pond $= \dots \times \dots$

$= \dots$ m^2

Area of path $= \dots - \dots$

$= \dots$ m^2

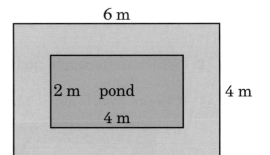

6 m

2 m pond 4 m

4 m

W 8 **7** Find the area of these triangles.
Set out your working clearly, as shown for the first triangle.

a Area of triangle $= \dfrac{\text{base} \times \text{height}}{2}$

$= \dfrac{6 \times 5}{2}$

$= \dots$ m^2

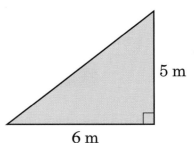

5 m

6 m

b

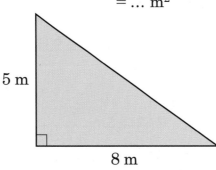

5 m

8 m

13 Statistics: getting it together

QUESTIONS

Crazy Cricket Calculations

Frank and Paul play for the same cricket team.

In the first half of the season, Frank averaged more runs per innings than Paul. He hoped he might win the trophy for the best batting average of the season.

Frank's average for the second half of the season was also better than Paul's.

Think how upset Frank was when he found out that Paul's average for the **whole** season was the best, so Paul won the trophy!

How could this happen?

1   Averages – mean, mode and median

How do we decide what is average?

◀◀ **REPLAY** ▶

There are 3 different types of average.

| mean |
| mode |
| median |

Perimeter   To find the **mean**:

(1) add up all the values,
(2) divide the total by the number of values given.

Example   The numbers of coloured pencils left in five packets are

3   5   1   6   5

Find the mean number of pencils in each packet.

The total of these values is $3 + 5 + 1 + 6 + 5 = 20$

There are 5 values.

Divide the total by the number of values $20 \div 5 = 4$

The **mean** is 4 pencils.

When 20 pencils are evenly shared between 5 packets, each packet has 4 pencils.

Exercise 13:1

1   Find the mean number of coloured pencils in these sets of packets.

a 3   1   6   2

b 3   1   2   2   3   1

c 6   4   11

d 8   5   4   3

^{G} 1, 2

The mean is not always a whole number.

Example   The numbers of coloured pencils left in 4 packets are

6   3   1   4

Find the mean number of pencils in each packet.

The total of these values is $6 + 3 + 1 + 4 = 14$

There are 4 values.

Divide the total by the number of values $14 \div 4 = 3.5$

The **mean** is 3.5 pencils.

Exercise 13:2

1   Find the mean number of coloured pencils in these sets of
packets.

a 3   1   4   2   2

b 8   3

c 6   3   3   2

d 5   3   2   0   4

2   You will need a calculator.
The table shows the cost of three items in four superstores.

	Store A	Store B	Store C	Store D
🍗	£3	£4	£3	£3.60
MENTOS	21 p	19 p	18 p	22 p
👕	£45	£52	£43	£40

a Find the mean price of a chicken.

b Find the mean price of a packet of mints.

c Find the mean price of a sports top.

d How many shops charged above the mean for a chicken?

e Which shops sold a packet of mints below the mean price?

f Which shop sold a sports top at exactly the mean price?

H1   **3** **a** **Without** using a ruler, estimate the length of these lines in centimetres.

Line A   Line B

Line C

Line D   Line E

b Work out the mean length using your estimates.

c Use a ruler to measure these lines exactly.
Write down the lengths.

d Work out the mean length using your measurements.

e Write down which mean is higher – the estimated one or the measured one.

4 Copy the sentence.

'People have a right to food and shelter.'

Write the number of letters in each word:

6   4   1   5   2   4   3   7

Work out the mean number of letters in a word.

5 Write down a sentence of your own.

a Underneath put the number of letters in each word.

b Work out the mean number of letters in a word.

Mode	The **mode** or the **modal value** is another form of average.
	The **mode** is the value that **occurs most often**.
	The mode is used to decide which record makes number 1 in the top ten.
	The record that is sold most often is 'Top of the Pops'.
Example	Find the mode from these numbers.
	3 1 2 1 1 2
	The number that occurs most often is 1. 1 is the **mode**.

Exercise 13:3

1 Find the mode from each set of numbers.

    a 5   1   2   1   2   2   **b** 3   4   2   4   1   4

For a very long list of numbers, use a **tally-table**.
For a shorter list, use a **stem diagram**.

Example   Find the modal number of pupils in a Year 8 tutor group.

Tutor group numbers are   28   27   27   29   28   27   29   25

To draw a **stem diagram**:

Write each of the numbers below a line
You only write a number once.

28	27	29	25

Put a dot above the line each time
the number occurs.

```
         •
  •      •      •
  •      •      •      •
 _____
 28     27     29     25
```

27 has the most dots.
27 occurs most often.
27 is the mode.
27 is the modal number of pupils in a Year 8 tutor group.

Exercise 13:4

For each question:

a Draw a line.

b Under the line write down each number in the list **once only**.

c Put a dot above the number each time it occurs.

d The number with the most dots is the mode.
   Write down the mode.

1 The number of sick pupils on eight days is

   3   15   0   3   1   0   4   3

2 The number of pupils forgetting homework on ten days is

   0   1   3   1   2   0   1   1   0   2

3 Ski boot sizes worn by sixteen pupils are

The mode does not have to be a number.

---

4 Crisp flavours chosen by seven pupils are

a Copy and complete
   the stem diagram.

b Which flavour of crisps is the mode?

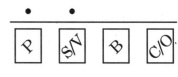

There can be more than one mode.

Example   Find the mode from the following numbers.

6   1   3   2   3   1   6   3   1

The numbers that occur most often are 1 and 3.
The mode is 1 **and** 3.

Exercise 13:5

For each question draw a stem diagram and find the mode.

1   5   1   5   3   1   3   2   5   2   1

2   6   8   7   8   5   7   6   8   7   8   7

3

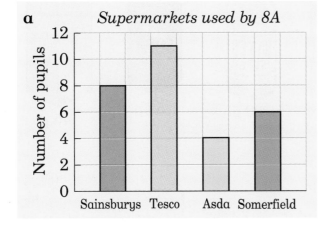

Modes can be worked out from charts and diagrams.

4   Look at each diagram.
The mode is the most popular choice.
Write down the mode for each diagram.

a   *Supermarkets used by 8A*

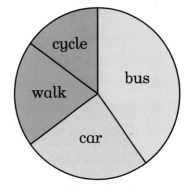

b   *How 8A come to school*

◄◄REPLAY►

| Median | The **median** is the **middle** value of data **after the values have been arranged in order of size.** |

Example

Manisha bought these school lunches in one week.

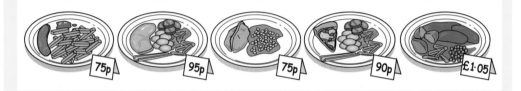

Find the median amount Manisha spent.

Put the amounts in order, cheapest first.

75 p   75 p   90 p   95 p   £1.05

The middle value is 90 p.
90 p is the median.

Exercise 13:6

1   Find the median price of these drinks.
First put them in order of price, cheapest first.

lemonade	milk	water	cola	orange
40 p	35 p	30 p	55 p	45 p

Copy and complete.

The middle value is . . . p

. . . p is the median.

2 Put the numbers in order, starting with the smallest.
Find the median of each of these sets of numbers.

a 7 5 6 7 4 8 3

b 14 16 17 12 13

c 35 37 29 21 38 36 32

d 0 4 0 2 8 5 1 7 9

3 Find the median price of these tennis rackets.

£55   £15   £85   £75   £30

4 Find the median weight of fish.

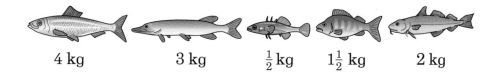

4 kg   3 kg $\frac{1}{2}$ kg $1\frac{1}{2}$ kg   2 kg

5 Find the median length of key.

8 cm   2 cm   4 cm   3 cm   5 cm

Sometimes there are two middle values.

Example   Find the median test mark.

| TEST Mark 14 | TEST Mark 10 | TEST Mark 16 | TEST Mark 12 | TEST Mark 18 | TEST Mark 20 |

Put the marks in order:

10   12   **14**   **16**   18   20

There are two middle values   **14** and **16**.

The median is exactly in the middle of **14** and **16**.

14 ◯ **16**   Sum $(14 + 16) \div 2 = 15$

The median is ⑮.

The median is 15.

Example   Find the median mark in the second test.

| TEST Mark 19 | TEST Mark 12 | TEST Mark 15 | TEST Mark 17 | TEST Mark 14 | TEST Mark 15 |

12   14   15   15   17   19

The two middle numbers are 15 and 15.

When the numbers are the same no sum is needed.

The median is 15.

Exercise 13:7

1 Find the median of these test results.
The marks have been put in order.

   a 3   5   6   6   7   8

   b 12   14   15   17   18   18

2 Put these marks in order first, then find the median.

   a 7   9   6   6   9   10

   b 38   31   34   36   37   36

   c 10   2   14   6   4   10

Which average?

New netball kit is needed but the team members can change each week.
Mrs Hill asks Gill, Fran and Serena to work out the average size of this team.

Exercise 13:8

1 Gill did the following things:
  (1) she measured all 7 heights in centimetres,
  (2) added the heights together,
  (3) divided the total by 7.

Gill's answer was 158 cm.
Which type of average did Gill find?

2 Fran did the following things:
  (1) she lined everyone up in order of height

  (2) measured only the middle one.

Fran's answer was 150 cm.
Which type of average did Fran use?

3 Serena did the following things:
  (1) she saw that 3 players were the same size

  (2) measured one of the three who were the same size.

Serena's answer was 145 cm.
Which type of average did Serena use?

Always say which average you are using.

4 The three average rates of pay per hour for workers at two sports shops are:

	Mean	Mode	Median
Sams Sports	£6	£5	£6
Top Shop	£8	£5	£7

a Liam works at Sams Sports. He wants a pay rise. Which average would Liam tell his boss about when asking for a pay rise?

b The boss at Sams Sports tells Liam that he pays average wages. Which average does his boss use?

5 The table below shows the wages per hour of each person working in a small business.

Position	Wages per hour in £s
Boss	50
Accountant	40
Salesperson	25
Secretary 1	10
Secretary 2	5
Receptionist	5
Cleaner	5

a Work out the total wages bill per hour.

b Work out the mean wage per hour.

c What is the mode wage?

d Work out the median wage.

e The boss wants you to think he pays good wages. Which average would he use?

f The boss wants his bank manager to think he is keeping costs down.
Which average would he use.

2 Range

◀◀REPLAY▶

Range	The **range** is the biggest value take away the smallest value.

The range tells us how spread out the values are.

Example   Find the range of lengths of time for these TV programmes.

60 mins   30 mins   20 mins   90 mins   40 mins

Draw a circle round the **biggest** value 90 minutes.

Draw a square round the **smallest** value 20 minutes.

Find the **range**   90 − 20 = 70 minutes

Exercise 13:9

Copy each of the following sets of data.

Draw a circle round the biggest value.
Draw a square round the smallest value.

Find the **range**   ◯ − ▢ = ...

1 Times in minutes of Tony's journeys to school.
25   21   24   26   21   24   26   27

2 The hours June spent watching TV in one week.
6   2   3   1 $2\frac{1}{2}$ 4   5

3 Amounts collected for Oxfam by Year 8 classes.
£12   £19   £20   £16   £14   £10   £15

4 The ages in years of people in one family.

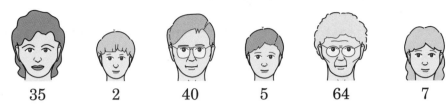

| 35 | 2 | 40 | 5 | 64 | 7 |

5 The heights in centimetres of people in another family.

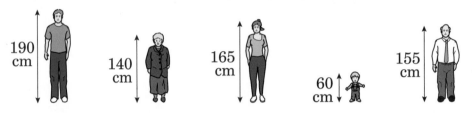

190 cm   140 cm   165 cm   60 cm   155 cm

Exercise 13:10   Handspan

W 1   You can use a piano or a keyboard worksheet (Worksheet 1).

Your task is to compare the number of white keys that can be reached on a piano by boys and girls.

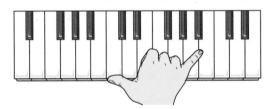

- How many white notes can you reach?
- You need to collect handspan data from 10 boys and 10 girls. You must keep the two sets of data separate.
- Draw diagrams to show the data for each set.
- Calculate different types of average for each set of data.
- Calculate the range for each set of data.
- Compare the results for the boys and for the girls using the diagrams and values you have worked out.
- Comment on your results.

- Collect a set of data of your own choice from boys and girls.
- Compare the results of the boys and of the girls.

3   Reading diagrams

Exercise 13:11

In January, Keep Fit Sportswear employed three new staff.

The graph shows their sales figures over the first six months.

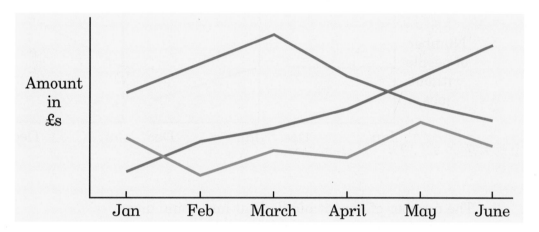

The sentences below describe their sales figures over the first six months.

Mr Potter's figures are up and down all the time.

Miss Khan started really well, but her figures are now dropping.

Mr McDonald started slowly, but his figures are going up all the time.

1   **a** Read the sentences carefully.

   b Look at the graph.

   c Copy the table below.

   d Write down each name next to the correct colour line.

		Name of member of staff
red		
green		
blue		

For each of these questions:

a Copy out the sentence.

b Choose which graph best matches the words.

c Draw the best graph next to the sentence and label it.

2 'The number of people without jobs is going up.'

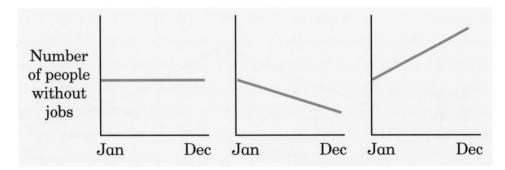

3 'The number of absent pupils is at last going down.'

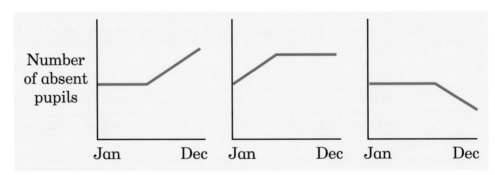

4 'This year Neesha's test results keep going up and down.'

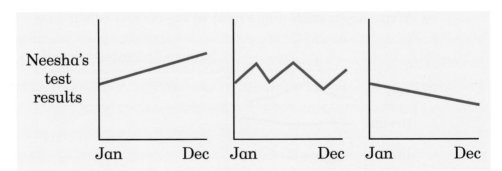

1 Find the mean number of sweets in a bag.

    a Number of sweets in each bag   5 7 1 4 3

    b Number of sweets in each bag   4 3 1 2

2 The stem diagram shows where families took their holidays.

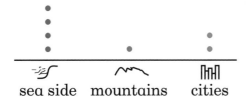

sea side mountains cities

    a Which holiday area is the mode?

    b Draw your own stem diagram to find the modal amount of money spent on holiday.

       £10 £20 £10 £5 £20 £15 £20 £10 £20

3 Find the median of these sets of numbers.
Remember to arrange them in order first.

    a 16 5 7 1 6 10 9

    b 4 1 8 6

4 Find the range for the baseball cap prices.

   £6   £12   £4   £8   £2   £9

5 Below each word is written the number of letters it contains.

    'One in fifteen people now own a mobile phone.'
      3   2   7   6   3   3   1   6   5

    a Find the mean number of letters in a word.

    b Find the median number of letters in a word.

c Find the modal number of letters in a word.

d Find the range.

e Which two averages give the same answer?

f Do you think a sentence in which the average number of letters in a word is 3 or 4 is easy or hard to read?

6 a Copy the sentence:

'Coming up to Christmas more money is spent on toys.'

b Draw and label the graph that best matches the sentence.

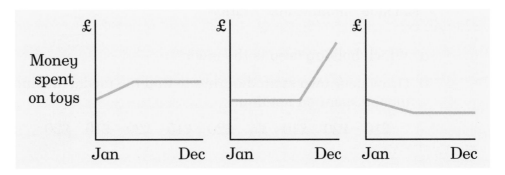

14 Volume: filling the space

QUESTIONS

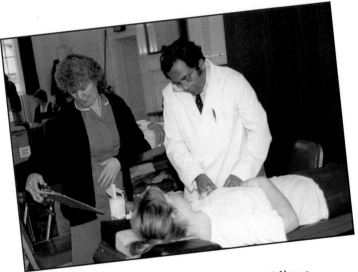

The average adult human female has 4.5 litres of blood in her body.

A male has slightly more.

If you give blood to the Blood Transfusion Service they take less than half a litre.

Altogether they collect 1.5 million litres each year.

This is the same as about 300 000 full bodies worth!

1 Pack it in!

The world record for the number of people in a phone box is 23. This is a lot of people in a very small space!

Volume	The amount of space that an object takes up is called its **volume**.

Example   A cereal box takes up more space than a matchbox.

The volume of the cereal box is **larger** than the volume of the matchbox.

Exercise 14:1

For each pair of objects write down which has the **larger** volume.

1

A sugar cube

A brick

2

A football

A table tennis ball

3

A tent

A house

Capacity	The capacity of a hollow object is the volume of space inside it. **Capacity** is usually used for liquids.
Example	A can of fizzy drink has a **smaller** capacity than a swimming pool.

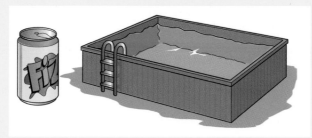

For each pair of objects write down which has the **smaller** capacity.

4

A milk bottle

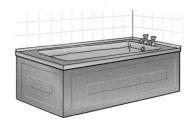

A bath

5

A milk tanker

A coffee mug

6

A carton of fruit juice

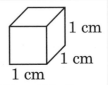

A bucket

G 1, 2

Measuring volume	Volume is measured using cubes.	
1 mm³	$1\,mm^3$ is the space taken up by one cube with all its edges 1 mm long.	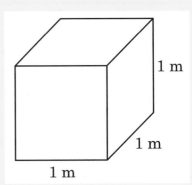
1 cm³	$1\,cm^3$ is the space taken up by one cube with all its edges 1 cm long.	
1 m³	$1\,m^3$ is the space taken up by one cube with all its edges 1 m long.	

For each pair of objects write down which has the **smaller** volume.

7 A box with volume $16\,\text{mm}^3$

A box with volume $16\,\text{cm}^3$

8 A box with volume $10\,\text{m}^3$

A box with volume $10\,\text{cm}^3$

9 A carton with volume $15\,\text{m}^3$

A carton with volume $15\,\text{mm}^3$

10 A carton with volume $75\,\text{cm}^3$

A box with volume $75\,\text{mm}^3$

 3, 4

| **Measuring capacity** | Capacity is measured using litres and millilitres. |

1 litre is the same as 1000 millilitres.

Litre is shortened to l.
Millilitre is shortened to ml.

This fruit juice carton holds 2 litres.   This milk carton holds 500 ml.

11 Look at these containers.
Write down the containers in order of capacity, **smallest** first.

Fizzy drink
330 ml

Shampoo
300 ml

Sauce bottle
220 ml

Yoghurt
100 ml

 5, 6

Estimating volume

W 1   This activity is for 2 people.

You need:
A 1 litre carton to help you.

This is what you do:

1   Collect as many different containers as you can.
You need at least seven.
Make sure they have the volume written on them.
Don't let the other person see the volumes on the containers.

     Some ideas for containers are:

     boxes of different sizes, bottles of different sizes,
cartons of different sizes.

2   Cut out pieces of scrap paper big
enough to cover the volumes.

3   Stick the pieces of paper over the
volume so they can be lifted up.

4   Swap containers with the other person.
No cheating! Don't try and look at the
volumes on the other containers.

5   Try to put the containers in order of volume in front of you.

6 Write down the name of each product on Worksheet 1.

Write down your estimate of the volume of each container. Decide which measurement to use from this list:

litres   millilitres   mm³   cm³   m³

Use the 1 litre container as a guide to help you.

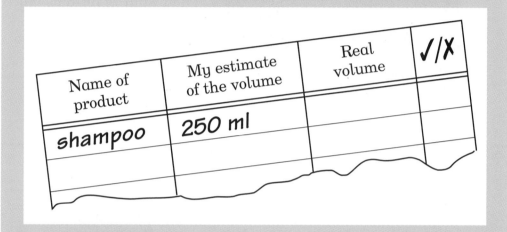

Name of product	My estimate of the volume	Real volume	✓/✗
shampoo	250 ml		

7 Lift the paper and write down the real volume of each container on your worksheet.

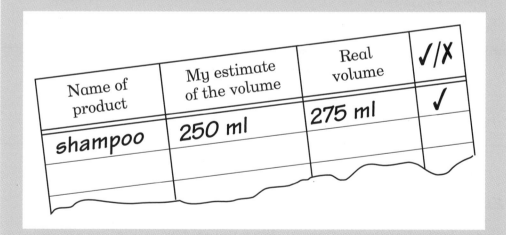

Name of product	My estimate of the volume	Real volume	✓/✗
shampoo	250 ml	275 ml	✓

8 Put a tick if your estimate is close and a cross if it is not close.

9 Stick your containers and worksheet on a large piece of paper to make a display for your classroom.

2 Stacking

Supermarkets stack their shelves so that you can see what they are selling.
They want to fit in as much as they can.
The shelf stackers need to work out how much they can fit in.

Example   Rachel is stacking cornflake boxes.

5 boxes fit **along** the shelf.

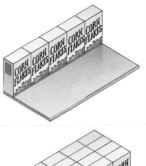

4 **rows** fit on the shelf.

$5 \times 4 = 20$ boxes

There are 20 boxes on the shelf.

Exercise 14:2

1   a How many boxes are **along** the shelf?

b How many rows are on the shelf?

c Copy the sum to find out how many boxes are on the shelf.

... × ... = ... boxes

2 a How many boxes are
along the shelf?

b How many rows are
on the shelf?

c Copy the sum to find out how many boxes are on the shelf.

... × ... = ... boxes

3 a How many boxes are
along the shelf?

b How many rows are
on the shelf?

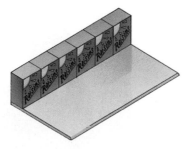

c Copy the sum to find out how many boxes are on the shelf.

... × ... = ... boxes

4 a How many boxes are
along the shelf?

b How many rows are
on the shelf?

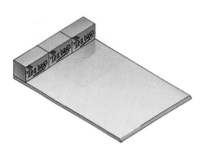

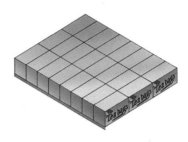

c Write a sum to find out how many boxes are on the shelf.

5 a How many boxes are
along the shelf?

b How many rows are
on the shelf?

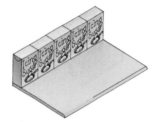

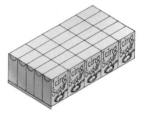

c Write a sum to find out how many boxes are on the shelf.

G 7, 8

Example   Ralph is making rectangles from blocks.

He has 6 rows of blocks.

Each row has 8 blocks.

$6 \times 8 = 48$ blocks

Ralph has used 48 blocks.

Exercise 14 : 3

You can use blocks to help you.

1 **a** How many blocks in a row?

   b How many rows?

   c How many blocks altogether?

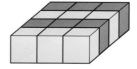

2 **a** How many blocks in a row?

   b How many rows?

   c How many blocks altogether?

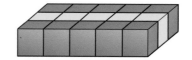

3 **a** How many blocks in a row?

   b How many rows?

   c How many blocks altogether?

4 **a** How many blocks in a row?

   b How many rows?

   c How many blocks altogether?

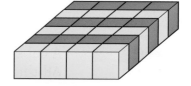

Exercise 14 : 4

Look at these pictures.
How many boxes are there in each picture?

1

2

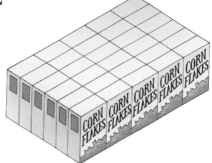

3

5

4

6

---

1 cm³   A cube that has sides of 1 cm is called a 1 cm cube.
All the edges are 1 cm long.

The volume of this cube is
1 cm cubed or **1 cm³**.

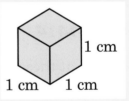

Example   This solid is made from 12 cubes.
It has a volume of 12 cm³.

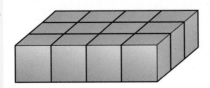

Exercise 14:5

Write down the volume of each arrangement of 1 cm cubes.

1

2
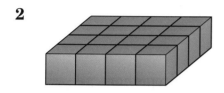

3

4
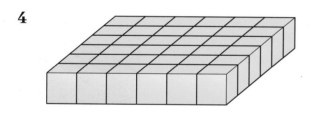

5
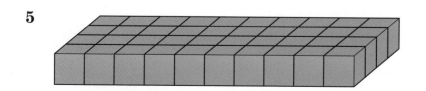

3 Stacking it higher

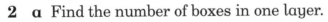

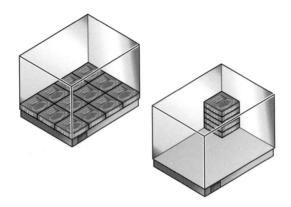

Rachel has to stack boxes of pizza in the freezer.

There are 3×4 pizzas in one layer.

There are 5 layers.

Rachel can fit in $3 \times 4 \times 5 = 60$ pizzas altogether.

Exercise 14:6

1 a Find the number of boxes in one layer.

 b Find the number of layers.

 c Copy and complete the sum to find the total number of boxes in the stack.

   $... \times ... \times ... = ...$ boxes

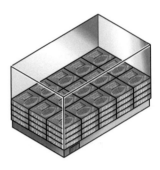

2 a Find the number of boxes in one layer.

 b Find the number of layers.

 c Copy and complete the sum to find the total number of boxes in the stack.

   $... \times ... \times ... = ...$ boxes

3 a Find the number of boxes in one layer.

 b Find the number of layers.

 c Copy and complete the sum to find the total number of boxes in the stack.

   $... \times ... \times ... = ...$ boxes

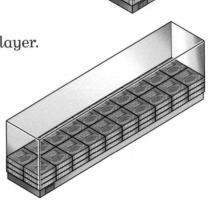

4 **a** Find the number of boxes in one layer.

  b Find the number of layers.

  c Copy the sum to find the total number of boxes in the stack.

 2

    ... × ... × ... = ... boxes

Example   Bethan has built this block out of 1 cm cubes.

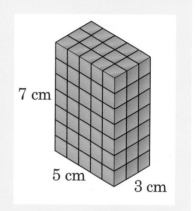

The length is 5 cm.

The width is 3 cm.

The height is 7 cm.

The volume is 5 cm × 3 cm × 7 cm = 105 cm³

Exercise 14:7

Find the volume of these blocks by multiplying. All the blocks are built out of 1 cm cubes.

 3 **1** Length = ... cm

    Width = ... cm

    Height = ... cm

    Volume = ... cm × ... cm × ... cm
    Volume = ... cm³

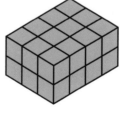

 3 **2** Length = ... cm

    Width = ... cm

    Height = ... cm

    Volume = ... cm × ... cm × ... cm
    Volume = ... cm³

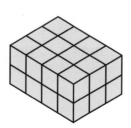

H 3   **3**   Length = … cm

Width = … cm

Height = … cm

Volume = … cm × … cm × … cm

Volume = … cm³

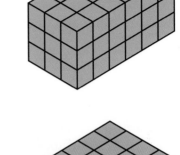

H 3   **4**   Length = … cm

Width = … cm

Height = … cm

Volume = … cm × … cm × … cm

Volume = … cm³

H 4   **5**   Length = … cm

Width = … cm

Height = … cm

Volume = … cm × … cm × … cm

Volume = … cm³

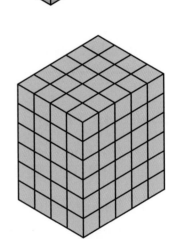

H 4   **6**   Length = … cm

Width = … cm

Height = … cm

Volume = … cm × … cm × … cm

Volume = … cm³

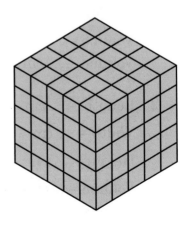

H 5   **7**   Length = ... cm

Width = ... cm

Height = ... cm

Volume = ... cm × ... cm × ... cm

Volume = ... cm³

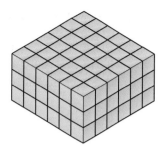

H 5   **8**   Length = ... cm

Width = ... cm

Height = ... cm

Volume = ... cm × ... cm × ... cm

Volume = ... cm³

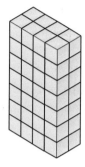

Exercise 14:8   *Building a box*

1   You need a piece of paper which measures 18 cm by 24 cm. You can use 1 cm squared paper.

Draw a square in each corner which measures 3 cm by 3 cm.

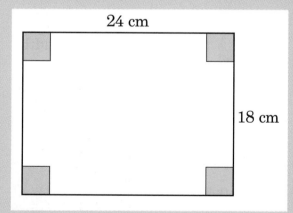

Cut the squares out.

Stick the edges together with sticky tape to make an open box.

Find the volume of
the box by measuring.

Length = ... cm

Width = ... cm

Height = ... cm

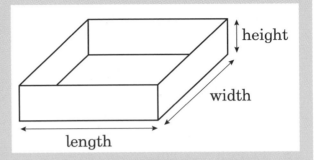

Volume = ... cm × ... cm × ... cm = ... cm^3

2 You need another piece of paper measuring 18 cm by 24 cm.
You can use 1 cm squared paper.

Draw a square in each
corner which measures
4 cm by 4 cm.

Cut the squares out.

Stick the edges
together to make
an open box.

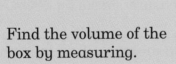

24 cm

18 cm

Find the volume of the
box by measuring.

Length = ... cm
Width = ... cm
Height = ... cm

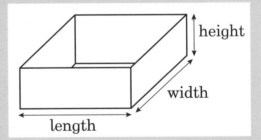

Volume = ... cm × ... cm × ... cm = ... cm^3

3 Make more boxes in the same way.

What is the biggest volume you can get?

4 Write a report of what you did and what you found out.

1 Which object has the **larger** volume?

   a A netball or a ping pong ball?

   b A toy car or a caravan?

2 Which has the **smaller** capacity?

   a A mug or a paddling pool?

   b A watering can or a teaspoon?

3 Which is the **smaller** volume?

   a $6\,m^3$ or $6\,cm^3$ **c** $8\,cm^3$ or $8\,mm^3$

   b $25\,mm^3$ or $25\,m^3$ **d** $20\,m^3$ or $10\,m^3$

4 **a** How many boxes are **along** the shelf?

   b How many rows are on the shelf?

   c Copy the sum to find out how many boxes are on the shelf.

     ... × ... = ... boxes

5 **a** How many blocks are in a row?

   b How many rows are there?

   c How many blocks are there altogether?

6 **a** How many blocks are in a row?

   b How many rows are there?

   c How many blocks are there altogether?

7 Write down the volume of each arrangement of 1 cm cubes.

a   **b**  **c**

8 a Find the number of cubes in one layer.

   b Find the number of layers.

   c Copy the sum to find the total number of cubes in the block.

   ... × ... × ... = ... cubes

9 Find the volume of these blocks by multiplying. They are all made from 1 cm cubes.

   a Length = ... cm

   Width = ... cm

   Height = ... cm

   Volume = ... cm × ... cm × ... cm

   Volume = ... cm³

   b Length = ... cm

   Width = ... cm

   Height = ... cm

   Volume = ... cm × ... cm × ... cm

   Volume = ... cm³

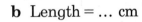

15 More or less?

QUESTIONS

A supertanker holds 300 000 tonnes of crude oil. This makes about 267 million litres of petrol.

A mini car covers about 13 km on 1 litre of petrol. The distance of the Sun from the Earth is about 150 million kilometres.

So Bill could drive his car to the Sun and back more than 11 times!

1   Trial and improvement

◀◀REPLAY▶

Josie tries to hit the target.
When a shot is too far to the left, the
next time she aims more to the right.
She is getting closer each time.

G 1, 2   Getting closer each time is called **trial and improvement**.

Example   To solve $x + 16 = 42$ by trial and improvement:
           (1) try different values of x until you get the answer 42
           (2) write your results in a table like this:

Possible value of x	Value of $x + 16$	Is the answer correct?
30	$30 + 16 = 46$	No – too big
25	$25 + 16 = 41$	No – just too small
26	$26 + 16 = 42$	Yes ✓

The answer is $x = 26$

Exercise 15 : 1

Find the value of x in these equations.
Use trial and improvement.

For each question:

a Draw a table.

b Fill it in.

c Keep trying until you get the correct answer.

d Write down the answer $x = \ldots$

H1 **1** $x + 13 = 52$

Possible value of x	Value of $x + 13$	Is the answer correct?
30	30 + 13 = 43	No – too small
40		.

Answer $x = \ldots$

H1 **2** $x + 24 = 65$

Possible value of x	Value of $x + 24$	Is the answer correct?
50	50 + 24 = 74	No – too big
40		

Answer $x = \ldots$

H1 **3** $x + 37 = 86$

Possible value of x	Value of $x + 37$	Is the answer correct?
40		

Answer $x = \ldots$

H2 **4** $x + 52 = 104$

Possible value of x	Value of $x + 52$	Is the answer correct?
50		

Answer $x = \ldots$

H 2   **5** $x + 17 = 52$

Possible value of x	Value of $x + 17$	Is the answer correct?

Answer $x = ...$

Example   You can use trial and improvement
                to solve any equation.

Solve $x - 15 = 38$

Possible value of x	Value of $x - 15$	Is the answer correct?
40	$40 - 15 = 25$	No – too small
50	$50 - 15 = 35$	No – still too small
55	$55 - 15 = 40$	No – too big
53	$53 - 15 = 38$	Yes ✓

Answer $x = 53$

Exercise 15:2

Use trial and improvement to solve these equations.
Write the answer $x = ...$

1 $x - 21 = 60$

Possible value of x	Value of $x - 21$	Is the answer correct?
90	$90 - 21 = 69$	No – too big
80		

2 $x - 32 = 36$

Possible value of x	Value of $x - 32$	Is the answer correct?
60	$60 - 32 = 28$	No – too small
70		

3 $x - 54 = 46$

Possible value of x	Value of $x - 54$	Is the answer correct?
90		

4 $x - 17 = 55$

Possible value of x	Value of $x - 17$	Is the answer correct?
80		

Sometimes there is more than one x in the equation.

Example Solve $2x + 21 = 35$

Possible value of x	Value of $2x + 21$	Is the answer correct?
4	$2 \times 4 + 21 = 29$	No – too small
6	$2 \times 6 + 21 = 33$	No – still too small
8	$2 \times 8 + 21 = 37$	No – too big
7	$2 \times 7 + 21 = 35$	Yes ✓

Answer $x = 7$

Exercise 15:3

Use trial and improvement to solve these equations.

4   **1** $2x + 24 = 36$

Possible value of x	Value of $2x + 24$	Is the answer correct?
8	$2 \times 8 + 24 = 40$	No – too big
5		

2 $2x + 48 = 70$

Possible value of x	Value of $2x + 48$	Is the answer correct?
10		

Now try these equations that have a take away sign.

3 $2x - 15 = 17$

Possible value of x	Value of $2x - 15$	Is the answer correct?
20	$2 \times 20 - 15 = 25$	No – too big
15		

4 $2x - 26 = 54$

Possible value of x	Value of $2x - 26$	Is the answer correct?
50		

2   Simple equations

◀◀REPLAY▶

Starting actions

Inverse actions

Each robot is paired with its inverse.
We can solve equations using inverses.

Inverse	An **inverse** is the action that returns you to where you started.

Example   Write down the inverse of **a** $+5$ and **b** $\times 7$

a start $+5$ **b** start $\times 7$

    inverse -5 inverse $\div 7$

Exercise 15:4

Write down the inverse of these actions.

 1 a $+4$ **b** $\times 2$ **c** $+10$ **d** $\div 7$

You can find the answers to equations using inverses.

Example   Solve the equation $x + 3 = 10$

The robot machine is $x \longrightarrow \boxed{+3} \longrightarrow 10$

The inverse machine is $x \longleftarrow \boxed{-3} \longleftarrow 10$

Look carefully at the direction of the arrows.
Answer $x = 7$

Check your answer: $x + 3 = 10$
$7 + 3 = 10$ correct ✓

Exercise 15:5

 Use the inverse machine to solve these equations.
Check your answers.

1 **a** $x + 4 = 17$ **b** $x + 5 = 27$

$x \longrightarrow \boxed{+4} \longrightarrow 17$ $x \longrightarrow \boxed{+5} \longrightarrow 27$

$\ldots \longleftarrow \boxed{-4} \longleftarrow 17$ $\ldots \longleftarrow \boxed{-5} \longleftarrow 27$

2 Solve these equations. Draw your own machines.
Check your answers.

  a $x + 9 = 23$ **b** $x + 6 = 15$ **c** $x + 5 = 24$ **d** $x + 11 = 20$

Example   Solve $x - 4 = 12$

Robot machine $x \longrightarrow \boxed{-4} \longrightarrow 12$

Inverse machine $x \longleftarrow \boxed{+4} \longleftarrow 12$

Answer $x = 16$ Check: $x - 4 = 12$
$16 - 4 = 12$ correct ✓

3 Use this method to solve these equations.

a $x - 17 = 3$

b $x - 6 = 18$

$x \longrightarrow \boxed{-17} \longrightarrow 3$

$\dots \longleftarrow \boxed{+17} \longleftarrow 3$

$x \longrightarrow \boxed{-6} \longrightarrow 18$

$\longleftarrow \boxed{} \longleftarrow 18$

Answer $x = \dots$

Check: $\dots - 17 = 3$

Answer $x = \dots$

Check: $\dots - 6 = 18$

 4 Draw your own machines to solve these equations in the same way.

a $x - 15 = 12$

b $x - 8 = 14$

An equation can be given in words.
You have to change the words into algebra and then solve it.

Example   I think of a number, add 5 and the answer is 12

Algebra $x + 5 = 12$

Machine

$x \longrightarrow \boxed{+5} \longrightarrow 12$

Inverse machine

$7 \longleftarrow \boxed{-5} \longleftarrow 12$

Answer $x = 7$
The number I thought of was 7.

---

 5 Change these words into algebra. Solve the equations using machines.

a I think of a number, add 6 and the answer is 18.

b I think of a number, take away 5 and the answer is 10.

Example Solve the equation $4x = 20$

Remember $4x$ means 4 times x or $x \times 4$

Machine

$$x \longrightarrow \boxed{\times 4} \longrightarrow 20$$

Inverse machine

$$x \longleftarrow \boxed{\div 4} \longleftarrow 20$$

Answer $x = 5$

Check: $4x = 20$

$5 \times 4 = 10$ Correct ✓

Exercise 15:6

1 Solve these equations using machines.

  a $4x = 12$ **b** $3x = 24$

     $x \times 4 = 12$ $x \times 3 = 24$

$$x \longrightarrow \boxed{\times 4} \longrightarrow 12 \qquad x \longrightarrow \boxed{\times 3} \longrightarrow 24$$

$$\ldots \longleftarrow \boxed{\div 4} \longleftarrow 12 \qquad \ldots \longleftarrow \boxed{\div 3} \longleftarrow 24$$

     Answer $x = \ldots$ Answer $x = \ldots$

     Check: $\ldots \times 4 = 12$ Check: $\ldots \times 3 = 24$

2 Draw your own machines to solve these equations.

  a $6x = 18$ **b** $4x = 48$ **c** $5x = 35$

     $x \times 6 = 18$ $x \times 4 = 48$ $x \times 5 = 35$

3 i Change these words into algebra and draw the machine.

 ii Draw the inverse machine to solve the equation.

  a Think of a number, call it x, multiply by 3 and the answer is 45. In algebra $x \times 3 = 45$.

  b Multiply x by 6 and the answer is 42.

  c Multiply x by 4 and the answer is 28.

Example   Solve the equation $\dfrac{x}{2} = 7$

Remember $\dfrac{x}{2}$ means $x \div 2$

Answer $x = 14$

Check: $x \div 2 = 7$
 $14 \div 2 = 7$ correct ✓

$$x \longrightarrow \boxed{\div 2} \longrightarrow 7$$

$$14 \longleftarrow \boxed{\times 2} \longleftarrow 7$$

Exercise 15:7

1 Solve these equations using machines.

a $\dfrac{x}{3} = 5$ **b** $\dfrac{x}{10} = 2$

$x \div 3 = 5$ $x \div 10 = 2$

$$x \longrightarrow \boxed{\div 3} \longrightarrow 5$$

$$\ldots \longleftarrow \boxed{\times 3} \longleftarrow 5$$

$$x \longrightarrow \boxed{\div 10} \longrightarrow 2$$

$$\ldots \longleftarrow \boxed{} \longleftarrow 2$$

Answer $x = \ldots$ Answer $x = \ldots$
Check: $\ldots \div 3 = 5$ Check: $\ldots \div 10 = 2$

2 Draw your own machines to solve these equations.

a $\dfrac{x}{4} = 3$ **b** $\dfrac{x}{5} = 4$ **c** $\dfrac{x}{2} = 12$

3 **i** Change these words into algebra and draw the machine.
ii Draw the inverse machine to solve the equation.

a Divide x by 4 and the answer is 2. In algebra $\dfrac{x}{4} = 2$.

b Divide x by 5 and the answer is 20.

c Divide x by 10 and the answer is 7.

Robot machines are also known as **function machines**.
A function machine can have 2 steps.

→ ×3 → +2 →

The inverse machine is:

← ÷3 ← −2 ←

Exercise 15:8

Draw the inverse function machines.

1 a → ×8 → −2 →

← ... ← ... ←

b → ÷3 → +1 →

← ... ← ... ←

c → ÷5 → −4 →

← ... ← ... ←

d → ×10 → −6 →

← ... ← ... ←

G 3, 4

Example Solve the equation $3x - 5 = 16$.

The machine is

$$x \longrightarrow \boxed{\times 3} \longrightarrow \boxed{-5} \longrightarrow 16$$

The inverse machine is

$$x \longleftarrow \boxed{\div 3} \longleftarrow \boxed{+5} \longleftarrow 16$$

Answer $x = 7$
Check: $3 \times 7 - 5 = 16$ correct ✓

Exercise 15:9

H 11 **1** Solve these equations using machines

a $3x - 7 = 23$
$\quad x \times 3 - 7 = 23$

$$x \longrightarrow \boxed{\times 3} \longrightarrow \boxed{-7} \longrightarrow 23$$

Answer $x = \ldots$
Check: $\ldots \times 3 - 7 = 23$

$$\ldots \longleftarrow \boxed{\div 3} \xleftarrow{30} \boxed{+7} \longleftarrow 23$$

b $2x + 12 = 24$
$\quad x \times 2 + 12 = 24$

$$x \longrightarrow \boxed{\times 2} \longrightarrow \boxed{+12} \longrightarrow 24$$

Answer $x = \ldots$
Check: $\ldots$

$$\ldots \longleftarrow \boxed{\ldots} \xleftarrow{\cdots} \boxed{\ldots} \longleftarrow 24$$

c $5x + 10 = 50$
$\quad x \times 5 + 10 = 50$

$$x \longrightarrow \boxed{\times 5} \longrightarrow \boxed{+10} \longrightarrow 50$$

Answer $x = \ldots$
Check: $\ldots$

$$\ldots \longleftarrow \boxed{\ldots} \xleftarrow{\cdots} \boxed{\ldots} \longleftarrow 50$$

d $7x - 6 = 29$
$\quad x \times 7 - 6 = 29$

$$x \longrightarrow \boxed{\times 7} \longrightarrow \boxed{-6} \longrightarrow 29$$

Answer $x = \ldots$
Check: $\ldots$

$$\ldots \longleftarrow \boxed{\ldots} \xleftarrow{\cdots} \boxed{\ldots} \longleftarrow 29$$

3 Range of numbers

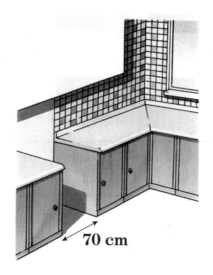

Mrs Jones is buying a new cooker.

The space is 70 cm wide.

70 cm

She wants to know which of these cookers will fit the space in her kitchen.

Cookers

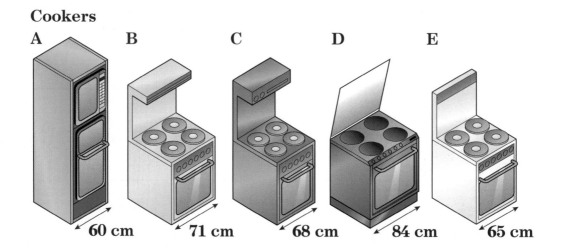

A	B	C	D	E
60 cm	71 cm	68 cm	84 cm	65 cm

A will fit because 60 cm is less than 70 cm.

B will not fit because 71 cm is more than 70 cm.

D will not fit because 84 cm is more than 70 cm.

W 1   **C** and **E** will also fit.

Exercise 15:10

1 Mr Khan is buying a new fridge.
It must fit in a space 150 cm **high**.
Which of these fridges will fit?

Refrigerators

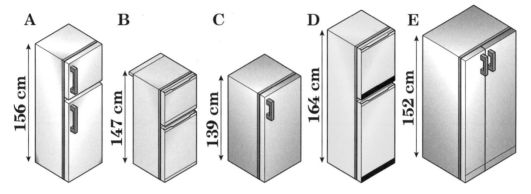

A 156 cm B 147 cm C 139 cm D 164 cm E 152 cm

2 Janina's bedroom window is 6.6 m from the ground.
She wants a safety ladder that she can use in case of fire.
These are the ladders in a catalogue.

SAFETY LADDERS	LADDER	LENGTH	PRICE
	A	3m	£25
	B	4m	£30
	C	8m	£50
	D	12m	£65
	E	20m	£100

a Which ladders would not reach the ground?

b Which ladder should she buy? Give your reasons.

Example The price of a Christmas tree depends on its height.

What is the cost of a tree of

a height 5 feet

b height $2\frac{1}{2}$ feet?

a Cost = £7
because 5 feet is
between 4 feet and 6 feet.

b Cost = £5
because $2\frac{1}{2}$ feet is
less than 4 feet.

Exercise 15:11

1 What is the cost of a Christmas tree of height:

    a 3 feet   **b** 8 feet   **c** $5\frac{1}{2}$ feet?

2 Barry is selling pumpkins for Halloween.

What is the cost of a pumpkin that weighs:

    a 3 kg   **c** 1.5 kg

    b 5 kg   **d** $2\frac{1}{2}$ kg?

3 On sports day points are given for the high jump.

Less than 80 cm	1 point
Between 80 cm and 100 cm	2 points
Between 100 cm and 120 cm	4 points
Over 120 cm	8 points

Work out the points for these pupils.

    a David 115 cm   **c** Charlene 122 cm

    b Peter 79 cm   **d** Kerri 81 cm

H 12   **1**   Solve $x + 18 = 54$ by trial and improvement.

Possible value of x	Value of $x + 18$	Is the answer correct?
30	30 + 18 =	
40		

Answer $x = \ldots$

H 12   **2**   Solve $2x + 42 = 78$ by trial and improvement.

Possible value of x	Value of $2x + 42$	Is the answer correct?
20	$2 \times 20 + 42 =$	

Answer $x = \ldots$

3   Write down the inverse of these numbers.

    a   +9   **b**   −7   **c**   ×8   **d**   ÷6

        ...   .

H 12   **4**   Use inverses to solve these equations.

    a $x + 9 = 27$ **b** $5x = 45$

$x \longrightarrow$ +9 $\longrightarrow 27$ $x \longrightarrow$ ×5 $\longrightarrow 45$

$\ldots \longleftarrow$ ... $\longleftarrow 27$ $\ldots \longleftarrow$ ... $\longleftarrow 45$

        Answer $x = \ldots$ Answer $x = \ldots$
        Check: $\ldots + 9 = 27$ Check: $\ldots \times 5 = 45$

5 Draw your own machines to solve these equations.

   a $x - 3 = 9$ **b** $\dfrac{x}{2} = 6$

                                          $x \div 2 = 6$

6 **i** Change these words into algebra.
     ii Draw your own machines to solve the equation.

    a Think of a number, call it x, take away 4 and the answer is 18.

    b Divide x by 4 and the answer is 10.

7 Draw the inverse machine.

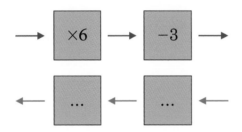

H 12   **8** Solve the equation $2x + 4 = 24$

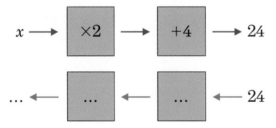

Answer $x = \ldots$
Check: $\ldots$

9 How much return bus fare must the following people pay?

    a Neesha – to travel 12 miles.

    b Sidney – to travel 4 miles.

    c Oliver – to travel 19 miles.

RETURN BUS FARES

0-5 miles	~ £1.50
6-10 miles	~ £2.00
11-15 miles	~ £3.00
16-20 miles	~ £4.00

QUESTIONS

Each symbol in the diagram has a value. The total values are placed alongside some rows and columns. What number should replace the question mark to give the value of the bottom row?

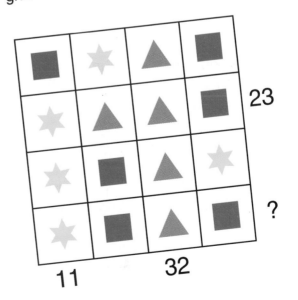

1 Drawing lines

◄◄REPLAY►

$$2 \longrightarrow \boxed{+5} \longrightarrow 7$$

If we put 6 into this robot we get:

$$6 \longrightarrow \boxed{+5} \longrightarrow 11$$

The robot adds 5 to any number we put in.

Exercise 16:1

Write down the answers to each of these questions.

1 **a** $1 \longrightarrow \boxed{+5} \longrightarrow ?$　　**3** **a** $10 \longrightarrow \boxed{-2} \longrightarrow ?$

　　b $3 \longrightarrow \boxed{+5} \longrightarrow ?$　　　　**b** $7 \longrightarrow \boxed{-2} \longrightarrow ?$

2 **a** $2 \longrightarrow \boxed{+7} \longrightarrow ?$　　**4** **a** $6 \longrightarrow \boxed{\times 2} \longrightarrow ?$

　　b $4 \longrightarrow \boxed{+7} \longrightarrow ?$　　　　**b** $2 \longrightarrow \boxed{\times 2} \longrightarrow ?$

G 1–6

Example　Use a $\boxed{+4}$ robot to find what answer you get if you start with 3.

$$3 \longrightarrow \boxed{+4} \longrightarrow ?$$

$$3 \longrightarrow \boxed{+4} \longrightarrow 7$$

The answer is 7.

5 What answer do you get from a +4 robot if you start with

   a 1   **b** 5   **c** 6?

6 What answer do you get from a ×3 robot if you start with

   a 2   **b** 5   **c** 10?

We can think of a +1 robot as

Input $x \longrightarrow$ +1 $\longrightarrow y$ **Output**

We start with x then add 1 to get y.
x can be any number we want.

Example   Use $x \longrightarrow$ +1 $\longrightarrow y$ to find the answer if

   a $x = 2$ **b** $x = 4$.

a If $x = 2$ **b** If $x = 4$

   $2 \longrightarrow$ +1 $\longrightarrow y$ $4 \longrightarrow$ +1 $\longrightarrow y$

   $2 \longrightarrow$ +1 $\longrightarrow 3$ $4 \longrightarrow$ +1 $\longrightarrow 5$

   So if $x = 2$, $y = 3$ So if $x = 4$, $y = 5$

---

7 Use $x \longrightarrow$ −3 $\longrightarrow y$ to find y if

   a $x = 7$ **b** $x = 5$ **c** $x = 8$

8 Use $x \longrightarrow$ ×10 $\longrightarrow y$ to find y if

   a $x = 3$ **b** $x = 4$ **c** $x = 2$

$x \longrightarrow \boxed{+2} \longrightarrow y$ is the same as $y = x + 2$

$x \longrightarrow \boxed{-5} \longrightarrow y$ is the same as $y = x - 5$

$x \longrightarrow \boxed{\times 2} \longrightarrow y$ is the same as $y = x \times 2$ (or $y = 2x$)

 7, 8

We can draw a line if we know the co-ordinates of at least two points on the line.

Example   Draw the line $y = x + 3$.

$y = x + 3$ is the same as

$x \longrightarrow \boxed{+3} \longrightarrow y$

Start with $x = 1$

$1 \longrightarrow \boxed{+3} \longrightarrow y$

If $x = 1$, then $y = 4$.
The co-ordinates are $(1, 4)$.

$1 \longrightarrow \boxed{+3} \longrightarrow 4$

Now use $x = 2$

$2 \longrightarrow \boxed{+3} \longrightarrow y$

If $x = 2$, then $y = 5$.
The co-ordinates are $(2, 5)$.

$2 \longrightarrow \boxed{+3} \longrightarrow 5$

Now use $x = 3$

$3 \longrightarrow \boxed{+3} \longrightarrow y$

If $x = 3$, then $y = 6$.
The co-ordinates are $(3, 6)$.

$3 \longrightarrow \boxed{+3} \longrightarrow 6$

1 We can plot the co-ordinates of the points $(1, 4)$, $(2, 5)$, $(3, 6)$ on the axes.

We start with $x = 1$, then $x = 2$, then $x = 3$, to give us points that are easy to work out and easy to plot on a grid.

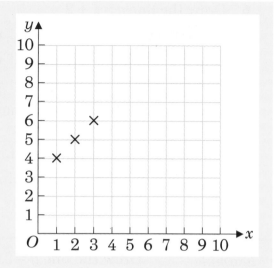

9

Exercise 16:2

1 Work out the co-ordinates of the points if

    a $x = 4$ **b** $x = 5$ **c** $x = 6$

2 Plot the points from the example and your answers to question **1** on the grid on Worksheet 1.

3 Draw a straight line through the points.

4 Label the line $y = x + 3$.

You only need two points to draw a line.
Other points are for checking.

---

2   **5** Use Worksheet 2 to draw the line $y = x + 4$.

    a Work out the co-ordinates if $x = 1$.
    b Plot the point on the grid.

    c Work out the co-ordinates if $x = 2$.
    d Plot the point on the grid.

    e Work out the co-ordinates if $x = 3$.
    f Plot the point on the grid.

    g Draw a line through the points.

    You should have a straight line.

    h Label the line $y = x + 4$.

H 1   **6**   Draw the line $y = x + 2$

     a Work out the co-ordinates if $x = 1$.

     b Work out the co-ordinates if $x = 2$.

     c Work out the co-ordinates if $x = 3$.

     d Draw a grid with x co-ordinates from 0 to 4 and y co-ordinates from 0 to 10.

     e Plot the points on your grid.

     f Draw a line through the points.

     g Label the line $y = x + 2$

Example   Draw the line $y = 3x$.

$y = 3x$ is the same as

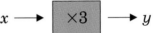

Start with $x = 1$
So if $x = 1$, then $y = 3$.
The co-ordinates are $(1, 3)$.

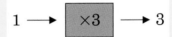

Now use $x = 2$
So if $x = 2$, then $y = 6$.
The co-ordinates are $(2, 6)$.

Now use $x = 3$
So if $x = 3$, then $y = 9$.
The co-ordinates are $(3, 9)$.

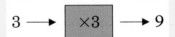

We can plot the co-ordinates
of the points $(1, 3)$, $(2, 6)$, $(3, 9)$
on the axes.
We draw a line through the points.
We label the line $y = 3x$.

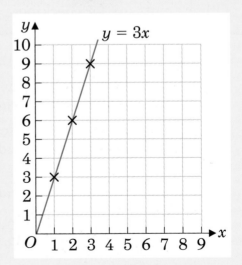

Exercise 16:3

 1 Draw the line $y = 2x$.

    a Work out the co-ordinates if $x = 1$.
    b Plot the point on the grid.

    c Work out the co-ordinates if $x = 2$.
    d Plot the point on the grid.

    e Work out the co-ordinates if $x = 3$.
    f Plot the point on the grid.

    g Draw a line through the points.

You should have a straight line.

    h Label the line $y = 2x$.

 2 Draw the line $y = 4x$.

    a Work out the co-ordinates if $x = 1$.

    b Work out the co-ordinates if $x = 2$.

    c Work out the co-ordinates if $x = 3$.

    d Draw a grid with x co-ordinates from 0 to 4 and y co-ordinates from 0 to 14.

    e Plot your points on your grid.

    f Draw a line through the points.

You should have a straight line.

    g Label the line $y = 4x$.

 3 **a** Draw a grid with x co-ordinates from 0 to 6 and y co-ordinates from 0 to 6.

    b Plot the points $(1, 1)$, $(2, 2)$, $(3, 3)$, $(4, 4)$, $(5, 5)$ on the grid.

    c Draw a line through the points with a ruler.

    d For each of these points:
        y co-ordinate $= x$ co-ordinate
        The line is $y = x$.
        Label the line $y = x$.

2   **Graphs of patterns**

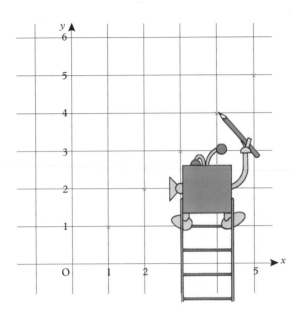

Exercise 16:4

1   Mr Swan lays matches in a pattern like this:

Pattern 1

Pattern 1 uses 4 matches.

Pattern 2   Pattern 3

a How many matches are used in pattern 2?

b How many matches are used in pattern 3?

c Draw pattern 4 and work out how many matches are used.

d Fill in the results table to show the number of matches used for patterns 1, 2, 3 and 4.

Pattern 1	Pattern 2	Pattern 3	Pattern 4	Pattern 5	Pattern 6
4	7	10	13	?	?

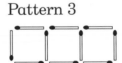

+?   +?   +?   +?   +?

e How many matches are added each time?

f How many matches would pattern 5 use?
Write the answer in the results table.

g How many matches would pattern 6 use?
Write the answer in the results table.

We can get co-ordinates from the results table.
Pattern 1 has co-ordinates (1, 4).
Pattern 2 has co-ordinates (2, 7).

h Fill in the gaps for the missing co-ordinates.

Pattern 3 has co-ordinates (3, ?).
Pattern 4 has co-ordinates (4, ?).
Pattern 5 has co-ordinates (?, ?).
Pattern 6 has co-ordinates (?, ?).

i Plot the points on the grid.
The first two points are plotted for you.
The points should be on a straight line.

Do not join up the points. It would not make sense.

2 Mr Green arranges tables and chairs like this:

1 table

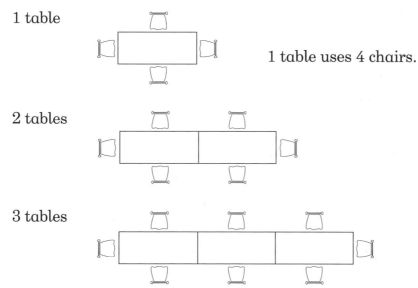

1 table uses 4 chairs.

2 tables

3 tables

a How many chairs are used with 2 tables?

b How many chairs are used with 3 tables?

c Draw the picture for 4 tables and work out how many chairs are used.

d Fill in the results table to show the number of chairs used for 1, 2, 3 and 4 tables.

1 table	2 tables	3 tables	4 tables	5 tables	6 tables
4	6	8	10	?	?

+?   +?   +?   +?   +?

e How many chairs are added each time?

f How many chairs would 5 tables use?
Write the answer in the results table.

g How many chairs would 6 tables use?
Write the answer in the results table.

We can get co-ordinates from the results table.
1 table has co-ordinates $(1, 4)$.
2 tables has co-ordinates $(2, 6)$.

h Fill in the gaps for the missing co-ordinates.

3 tables has co-ordinates $(3, ?)$.
4 tables has co-ordinates $(4, ?)$.
5 tables has co-ordinates $(?, ?)$.
6 tables has co-ordinates $(?, ?)$.

i Plot the points on the grid.
The first point is plotted for you.
The points should be on a straight line.

Do not join up the points.
It would not make sense.

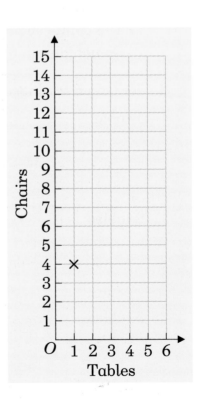

3 Solving puzzles

Exercise 16:5

1 A number pattern starts like this:

First				Second				Third		
2	3	4		5	6	7		8	9	10

a Write down the fourth and fifth parts of the pattern.

Here are some more parts of the same pattern.
Copy them and fill in the missing numbers.

b

11	?	13

e

50	51	?

c

17	18	?

f

68	?	70

d

?	21	22

g

?	84	85

2 Here is another pattern.

First	
2	3
4	5

Second	
5	6
7	8

Third	
8	9
10	11

a Draw the next two parts of the pattern.

Here are some more parts of the same pattern.
Copy the squares and fill in the missing numbers.

b

14	...
16	...

c

17	...
...	20

d

...	21
...	23

3 Here is another pattern.

2	4
6	8

8	♥
12	14

14	♠
♣	20

Write down the value of   **a** ♥   **b** ♠   **c** ♣

Example   Here is John's newspaper problem.

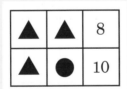

This means:

▲ + ▲ = 8

▲ + ● = 10

The two triangles add up to 8. One triangle must be 4.

One triangle and one circle add up to 10. One circle
must be 6 because 4 + 6 = 10.

Exercise 16:6

1 Find how much each shape is worth in each of these puzzles.

a

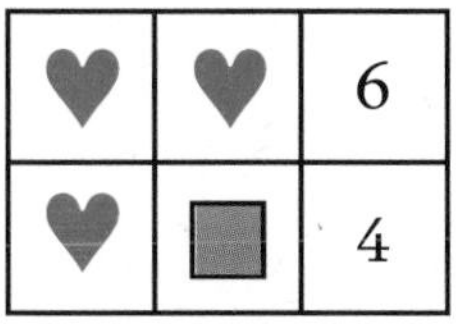

♥	♥	6
♥	■	4

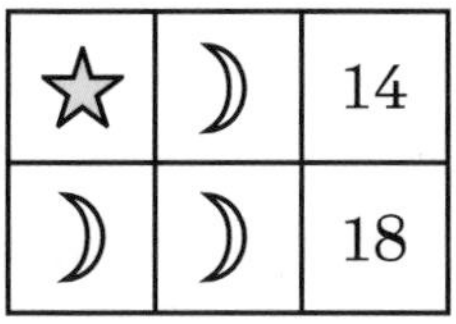

e

🍎	🍎	🍎	9
🍎	🍎	□	7

b

●	●	8
△	●	6

f

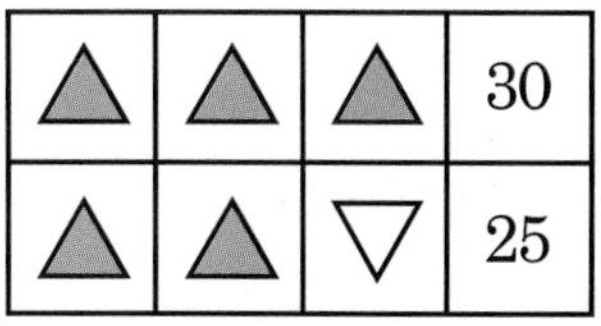

△	△	△	30
△	△	▽	25

c

■	■	14
■	◇	9

g

A	B	B	24
A	A	A	12

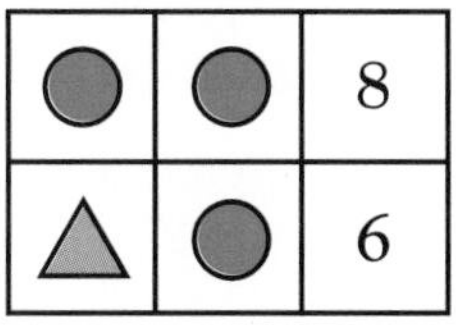

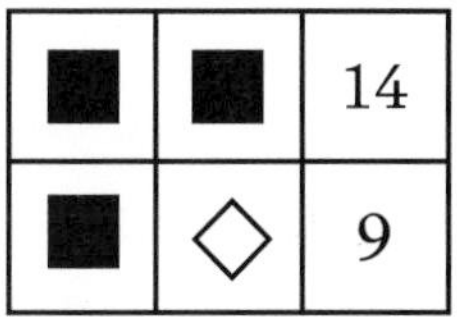

d

☆	☽	14
☽	☽	18

h

□	□	□	3
♥	□	♥	5

297

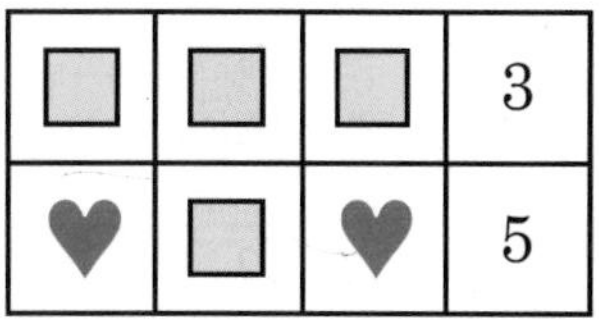

1 Write down the answers to each of these questions.

a $3 \longrightarrow \boxed{+3} \longrightarrow ?$ **f** $6 \longrightarrow \boxed{\times 10} \longrightarrow ?$

b $5 \longrightarrow \boxed{+3} \longrightarrow ?$ **g** $3 \longrightarrow \boxed{\times 10} \longrightarrow ?$

c $12 \longrightarrow \boxed{-2} \longrightarrow ?$ **h** $6 \longrightarrow \boxed{\div 2} \longrightarrow ?$

d $9 \longrightarrow \boxed{-2} \longrightarrow ?$ **i** $10 \longrightarrow \boxed{\div 2} \longrightarrow ?$

e $4 \longrightarrow \boxed{-2} \longrightarrow ?$ **j** $16 \longrightarrow \boxed{\div 2} \longrightarrow ?$

2 What answer do you get from a $\boxed{\times 5}$ robot if you start with

a 1   **b** 2   **c** 3   **d** 4?

3 Use $x \longrightarrow \boxed{-3} \longrightarrow y$ to find y if

a $x = 10$ **b** $x = 5$ **c** $x = 3$ **d** $x = 6$

4 $x \longrightarrow \boxed{+2} \longrightarrow y$ is the same as $y = x + 2$.

What are these robots the same as?

a $x \longrightarrow \boxed{+3} \longrightarrow y$ **d** $x \longrightarrow \boxed{\times 3} \longrightarrow y$

b $x \longrightarrow \boxed{-4} \longrightarrow y$ **e** $x \longrightarrow \boxed{-5} \longrightarrow y$

c $x \longrightarrow \boxed{\times 2} \longrightarrow y$ **f** $x \longrightarrow \boxed{+8} \longrightarrow y$

5 **5** Draw the line $y = x + 5$.

    a Work out the co-ordinates if $x = 1$.

    b Work out the co-ordinates if $x = 2$.

    c Work out the co-ordinates if $x = 3$.

    d Draw a grid with x co-ordinates from 0 to 4 and y co-ordinates from 0 to 10.

    e Plot the points on your grid.

    f Draw a line through the points.

    g Label the line $y = x + 5$.

6 **6** Draw the line $y = 5x$.

    a Work out the co-ordinates if $x = 1$.

    b Work out the co-ordinates if $x = 2$.

    c Work out the co-ordinates if $x = 3$.

    d Draw a grid with x co-ordinates from 0 to 4 and y co-ordinates from 0 to 16.

    e Plot the points on your grid.

    f Draw a line through the points.

    g Label the line $y = 5x$

7 **7** Miss Swan lays matches in a pattern like this:

Pattern 1   Pattern 2   Pattern 3

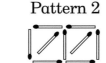 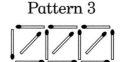

Pattern 1 uses 5 matches.

    a How many matches are used in pattern 2?

    b How many matches are used in pattern 3?

    c Draw pattern 4 and work out how many matches are used.

    d Fill in the results table to show the number of matches used for patterns 1, 2, 3 and 4.

Pattern 1	Pattern 2	Pattern 3	Pattern 4

e How many matches are added each time?

f Pattern 1 has co-ordinates $(1, 5)$.
Write down the co-ordinates for each pattern.

g Draw a grid with x co-ordinates from 0 to 4
and y co-ordinates from 0 to 20.

h Plot the points on the grid.
Do not join the points up.

8 a Copy this pattern. Fill in the missing numbers.

1	2	3		7	8	9		?	14	?
	4	5	6		?	11	12			

b Here is another pattern.
Write down the value of each letter.

1	2	3		a	6	7		9	c	11
	3	4	5		7	8	b		d	

9 Find how much each shape is worth on each of these puzzles.

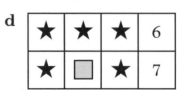

a

□	□	2
□	●	5

c

▲	▲	10
○	▲	15

b

♥	△	5
♥	♥	4

d

★	★	★	6
★	▢	★	7

+ **add   total   sum   plus** +

There are different ways of writing the same sum.

Example

Sum   13 + 2 = **15**

can be set out in columns

```
    T U
    1 3
  +   2
  ─────
    1 5
```

or written using words:

> 13 **add** 2 is **15**.
> The **total** of 13 and 2 is **15**.
> The **sum** of 13 and 2 is **15**.
> 13 **plus** 2 is **15**.

Copy these sums into your book.
You can use columns.
Work out the answers.

Exercise 1

1   1 6
      +   3
      ─────

2   2 4
       + 3 2
       ─────

3 36 + 12

4 32 add 26

5 The total of
      27 and 21

6 The sum of
      47 and 42

Exercise 2

1 52 plus 34

2 The total of
      18 and 31

3 64 + 35

4 The sum of
      51 and 8

5   1 5
       + 3 3
       ─────

6   4 6
       + 2 3
       ─────

Exercise 3

1 63 add 14

2   2 6
       + 5 3
       ─────

3 84 plus 13

4 21 + 6

5 The sum of
      71 and 26

6   5 5
       + 4 2
       ─────

When a column adds up to 10 or more we need to **carry**.

Example

1 Sum $13 + 9$

$$3 + 9 = 12$$
1 ten and 2 units

```
  T U
  1 3
+   9
  ───
  2 2
  ─
  1
carry
```

2 Sum $27 + 29$

$$7 + 9 = 16$$
1 ten and 6 units

```
  T U
  2 7
+ 2 9
  ───
  5 6
  ─
  1
carry
```

Copy these sums into your book.
You can use columns.
Work out the answers.

Exercise 4

1
```
  1 8
+   6
───
```

2
```
  3 4
+ 2 8
───
```

3 $47 + 36$

4 The total of
53 and 19

5 $68 + 7$

6 The sum of
27 and 44

Exercise 5

1 38 plus 27

2 16 add 46

3 $69 + 35$

4 The total of
25 and 37

5
```
  7 7
+ 3 6
───
```

6
```
  8 3
+ 1 8
───
```

Exercise 6

1 $33 + 57$

2
```
  2 6
+ 5 8
───
```

3 45 plus 48

4 89 add 9

5
```
  3 8
+ 2 8
───
```

6 The sum of
25 and 69

take away subtract minus difference

There are different ways of writing subtraction sums.

Example

Sum $28 - 10 = 18$

can be set out in columns

```
  T U
  2 8
- 1 0
  ___
  1 8
```

or written using words:

28 **take away** 10 is **18**.
Subtract 10 from 28. Answer **18**.
28 **minus** 10 is **18**.
The **difference** between 10 and 28 is **18**.

Copy these sums into your book.
You can use columns.
Work out the answers.

Exercise 7

1
```
  2 9
- 1 6
  ___
```

2
```
  5 6
- 2 3
  ___
```

3 $45 - 31$

4 68 take away 22

5 74 minus 51

6 Subtract 11 from 29

Exercise 8

1 The difference between 12 and 36

2 $57 - 24$

3 Subtract 13 from 48

4 64 minus 10

5
```
  8 9
- 6 8
  ___
```

6 $37 - 22$

Exercise 9

1 26 take away 5

2 $49 - 32$

3 Subtract 45 from 69

4
```
  9 8
- 3 4
  ___
```

5 The difference between 35 and 15

6 $76 - 51$

When the **bottom** digit is **bigger** than the **top** digit change a ten to units.

Example

a Find 42 − 19

$$\begin{array}{cc} \text{T} & \text{U} \\ 4 & 2 \\ -1 & 9 \\ \hline \end{array}$$ ⟶ $$\begin{array}{cc} \text{T} & \text{U} \\ {}^3\!\!\!\diagup\!4 & {}^1 2 \\ -1 & 9 \\ \hline \end{array}$$ ⟶ Take 9 from 12
Take 1 from 3
$$\begin{array}{cc} \text{T} & \text{U} \\ {}^3\!\!\!\diagup\!4 & {}^1 2 \\ -1 & 9 \\ \hline 2 & 3 \end{array}$$

b Find 64 − 28

$$\begin{array}{cc} \text{T} & \text{U} \\ 6 & 4 \\ -2 & 8 \\ \hline \end{array}$$ ⟶ $$\begin{array}{cc} \text{T} & \text{U} \\ {}^5\!\!\!\diagup\!6 & {}^1 4 \\ -2 & 8 \\ \hline \end{array}$$ ⟶ $$\begin{array}{cc} \text{T} & \text{U} \\ {}^5\!\!\!\diagup\!6 & {}^1 4 \\ -2 & 8 \\ \hline 3 & 6 \end{array}$$

Copy these sums into your book.
You can use columns.
Work out the answers.

Exercise 10

1　$\begin{array}{cc} 3 & 2 \\ -1 & 8 \\ \hline \end{array}$

2　$\begin{array}{cc} 4 & 2 \\ -2 & 7 \\ \hline \end{array}$

3 31 − 19

4 43 take away 29

5 64 minus 38

6 Subtract 14 from 51

Exercise 11

1 The difference between 8 and 22

2 65 − 37

3 41 minus 16

4 54 take away 26

5　$\begin{array}{cc} 8 & 6 \\ -4 & 9 \\ \hline \end{array}$

6 70 − 45

Exercise 12

1 33 − 9

2 Subtract 77 from 93

3　$\begin{array}{cc} 5 & 0 \\ -2 & 6 \\ \hline \end{array}$

4 The difference between 28 and 42

5 81 minus 59

6 Subtract 25 from 72

add + carry   take away – borrow

Copy these sums into your book.
You can use columns.
Work out the answers.

Exercise 13

1
```
   6 7
 + 2 2
 -----
```

2
```
   2 9
 - 1 5
 -----
```

3
```
   4 3
 +   6
 -----
```

4
```
   3 7
 -   4
 -----
```

5
```
   5 6
 + 3 5
 -----
```

6
```
   7 2
 - 2 8
 -----
```

7
```
   1 9
 + 6 8
 -----
```

8
```
   4 5
 - 2 9
 -----
```

Exercise 14

1 34 add 25

2 The sum of 17 and 13

3 48 minus 11

4 Subtract 23 from 85

5 The total of 56 and 16

6 The difference between 41 and 18

7 64 + 27

8 33 – 17

9 43 plus 27

10 The sum of 9 and 58

11 The difference between 14 and 60

12 29 + 39

Copy these sums into your book.
Write down the answers.

Exercise 15	Exercise 16	Exercise 17	Exercise 18
1 2×2	1 3×4	1 2×5	1 3×2
2 4×6	2 8×6	2 7×5	2 7×6
3 8×5	3 3×9	3 9×4	3 3×6
4 2×4	4 6×6	4 3×3	4 7×4
5 2×9	5 5×4	5 2×8	5 3×5
6 5×5	6 2×7	6 4×3	6 5×2
7 2×3	7 4×5	7 5×6	7 4×4
8 8×4	8 7×4	8 3×7	8 2×6
9 6×5	9 6×3	9 6×4	9 9×5
10 3×8	10 4×2	10 9×6	10 6×2

× multiply times product ×

Example

$31 \times 5 = \mathbf{155}$

When we are adding lots of the same number it is quicker to multiply.

```
   3 1
   3 1
   3 1     is the same as           3 1
   3 1                            ×   5    This way is quicker.
 + 3 1                            1 5 5
 ─────
 1 5 5
```

To do
```
   3 1     first do 5 × 1     3 1     then do 5 × 3     3 1
 ×   5                      ×   5                     ×   5
 ─────                      ─────                     ─────
                                5                     1 5 5
```

31 **multiplied** by 5 is **155**.
31 **times** 5 is **155**.
The **product** of 31 and 5 is **155**.

Copy these sums into your book.
Use the quicker way to work out the answers.

Exercise 19

1
```
    2 3
  ×   2
  ─────
```

2 51×9

3 42 multiplied by 3

4 22 times 4

5
```
    2 4
  ×   2
  ─────
```

6 The product of 43 and 3

Exercise 20

1
```
    5 2
  ×   4
  ─────
```

2 62×3

3 21 multiplied by 5

4 33 times 2

5
```
    3 4
  ×   2
  ─────
```

6 The product of 41 and 4

Exercise 21

1
```
    1 3
  ×   3
  ─────
```

2 32×2

3 52 multiplied by 4

4 41 times 3

5
```
    4 4
  ×   2
  ─────
```

6 The product of 61 and 5

Sometimes we need to carry in multiplying.

Example

1 26×3

$$
\begin{array}{r}
2\ 6 \\
\times\ \ 3 \\
\hline
8 \\
\end{array}
\ {\scriptstyle 1}
\qquad \longrightarrow \qquad
\begin{array}{r}
2\ 6 \\
\times\ \ 3 \\
\hline
7\ 8 \\
\end{array}
\ {\scriptstyle 1}
$$

$3 \times 2 = 6$
Then add the **1** to give **7**

Example

2 114×6

$$
\begin{array}{r}
1\ 1\ 4 \\
\times\ \ \ \ 6 \\
\hline
4 \\
\end{array}
\ {\scriptstyle 2}
\ \longrightarrow\
\begin{array}{r}
1\ 1\ 4 \\
\times\ \ \ \ 6 \\
\hline
8\ 4 \\
\end{array}
\ {\scriptstyle 2}
\ \longrightarrow\
\begin{array}{r}
1\ 1\ 4 \\
\times\ \ \ \ 6 \\
\hline
6\ 8\ 4 \\
\end{array}
\ {\scriptstyle 2}
$$

$6 \times 1 = 6$
Then add the **2** to give **8**

Copy these sums into your book.
Work out the answers.

Exercise 22	**Exercise 23**	**Exercise 24**

Exercise 22

1 $\begin{array}{r} 1\ 2 \\ \times\ \ 6 \\ \hline \end{array}$

2 $\begin{array}{r} 2\ 2\ 3 \\ \times\ \ \ \ 4 \\ \hline \end{array}$

3 245×2

4 38 times 2

5 The product of 224 and 3

6 328 multiplied by 3

Exercise 23

1 $\begin{array}{r} 3\ 4 \\ \times\ \ 3 \\ \hline \end{array}$

2 $\begin{array}{r} 3\ 2\ 8 \\ \times\ \ \ \ 2 \\ \hline \end{array}$

3 216×4

4 46 times 2

5 The product of 311 and 4

6 324 multiplied by 3

Exercise 24

1 $\begin{array}{r} 2\ 4 \\ \times\ \ 3 \\ \hline \end{array}$

2 $\begin{array}{r} 1\ 1\ 4 \\ \times\ \ \ \ 5 \\ \hline \end{array}$

3 124×3

4 52 times 3

5 The product of 212 and 6

6 128 multiplied by 3

× multiplying by 10 and 100 ×

When we **multiply by 10**, all the digits move across **one** column to the **left**.
This makes the number 10 times bigger.

Example

1 23 × 10 = 230

```
  H   T   U
      2   3
  2   3   0
```
×10 ×10

When we **multiply by 100**, all the digits move across **two** columns to the **left**.
This makes the number 100 times bigger.

Example

2 74 × 100 = 7400

```
 Th  H   T   U
         7   4
  7  4   0   0
```
×100 ×100

Exercise 25

Multiply these numbers by 10.

1 39

2 45

3 72

4 83

5 55

6 128

7 756

8 684

9 251

10 367

Exercise 26

Multiply these numbers by 100.

1 75

2 82

3 33

4 59

5 20

6 178

7 420

8 818

9 302

10 400

Exercise 27

Copy these sums into your book.
Write down the answers.

1 76 × 10

2 31 × 100

3 54 × 100

4 99 × 10

5 25 × 10

6 131 × 10

7 284 × 100

8 354 × 10

9 831 × 100

10 90 × 10

$$68 \div 2 \qquad \frac{68}{2} \qquad \text{divide 68 by 2} \qquad \text{share 68 between 2}$$

Example

1 $68 \div 2$

$2\overline{)68}$ First work out $6 \div 2 = 3$

$\overset{3}{2\overline{)68}}$ Put the 3 above the 6.

$\overset{34}{2\overline{)68}}$ Now work out $8 \div 2 = 4$
Put the 4 above the 8.

So $68 \div 2 = 34$

Example

2 Divide 80 by 4.

$4\overline{)80}$ First work out $8 \div 4 = 2$

$\overset{2}{4\overline{)80}}$ Put the 2 above the 8.

$\overset{20}{4\overline{)80}}$ Now work out $0 \div 4 = 0$
Put the 0 above the 0.

So $68 \div 2 = 34$

Exercise 28

Work these out:

1 $2\overline{)84}$

2 $\dfrac{93}{3}$

3 $55 \div 5$

4 Divide 96 by 3

5 $4\overline{)48}$

6 Share 64 between 2

Exercise 29

Work these out:

1 $\dfrac{69}{3}$

2 $48 \div 2$

3 Share 60 between 3

4 $6\overline{)66}$

5 Divide 24 by 2

6 $3\overline{)96}$

Exercise 30

Work these out:

1 Divide 62 by 2

2 $3\overline{)39}$

3 Share 60 between 6

4 $84 \div 4$

5 $\dfrac{50}{5}$

6 $82 \div 2$

Dividing when we need to 'carry'

Sometimes we need to 'carry'.
This happens when a number does not divide exactly.

Example

1 $64 \div 4$

$4\overline{)64}$ — First do $6 \div 4$. This is 1 with 2 left over.

$4\overline{)6^24}$ with 1 above — Put the 1 above the 6 and carry the 2.

$4\overline{)6^24}$ with $1\ 6$ above — Now do $24 \div 4$. This is 6.
Put the 6 above the 4.

So $64 \div 4 = 16$

Example

2 Share 75 between 5.

$5\overline{)75}$ — First do $7 \div 5$. This is 1 with 2 left over.

$5\overline{)7^25}$ with 1 above — Put the 1 above the 7 and carry the 2.

$5\overline{)7^25}$ with $1\ 5$ above — Now do $25 \div 5$. This is 5.
Put the 5 above the 5.

So $75 \div 5 = 15$

Exercise 31

Work these out.

1 $2\overline{)52}$

2 $3\overline{)45}$

3 $\dfrac{56}{4}$

4 Divide 72 by 6

5 Share 65 between 5

6 $75 \div 3$

Exercise 32

Work these out.

1 $42 \div 3$

2 Divide 52 by 4

3 $2\overline{)34}$

4 Share 84 between 6

5 $3\overline{)54}$

6 $\dfrac{60}{5}$

Exercise 33

Work these out.

1 $36 \div 2$

2 Share 48 between 3

3 $\dfrac{80}{5}$

4 Divide 60 by 4

5 $6\overline{)96}$

6 $72 \div 3$

Dividing by 10

When we **divide by 10**, all the digits move across **one** column to the **right**.
This makes the number smaller.

Example

$230 \div 10 = 23$

H	T	U
2	3	0

$\div 10$ $\div 10$

2   3

Here are some more examples.

T	U
8	0

$\div 10$

8    $80 \div 10 = 8$

Th	H	T	U
2	4	6	0

$\div 10$ $\div 10$ $\div 10$

2   4   6 $2460 \div 10 = 246$

Dividing by 100

When we **divide by 100**, all the digits move across **two** columns to the **right**. This is because $100 = 10 \times 10$. So dividing by 100 is like dividing by 10 twice.

Example

$7400 \div 100 = 74$

Th	H	T	U
7	4	0	0

$\div 100$ $\div 100$

7   4

Here is another example.

Th	H	T	U
5	3	0	0

$\div 100$ $\div 100$

5   3 $5300 \div 100 = 53$

Exercise 34

Divide these numbers by 10.

1 370

2 90

3 450

4 3540

5 20

6 590

7 4720

8 650

Exercise 35

Divide these numbers by 100.

1 5200

2 4300

3 8500

4 9200

5 7400

6 3700

7 4800

8 6700

Exercise 36

Work these out.

1 $750 \div 10$

2 $3200 \div 100$

3 $6700 \div 100$

4 $3200 \div 10$

5 $7500 \div 100$

6 $4360 \div 10$

7 $5360 \div 10$

8 $4200 \div 100$

multiply × times   divide ÷ share

Copy these sums into your book.
You can use columns.
Work out the answers.

Exercise 37

1 48 ÷ 2

2 27 multiplied by 4

3 $\dfrac{72}{4}$

4 The product of 13 and 5

5
$$\begin{array}{r} 2\ 6 \\ \times\ \underline{3} \\ \hline \end{array}$$

6 19 times 5

7 75 divided by 5

8 Share 18 by 3

9 14 × 5

10 Divide 52 by 2

11 54 ÷ 3

12 The product of 22 and 10

13 41 × 10

14 37 × 100

15 Share 98 between 2

Exercise 38

1 28 ÷ 2

2 33 multiplied by 4

3 $\dfrac{85}{5}$

4 The product of 10 and 12

5
$$\begin{array}{r} 3\ 2 \\ \times\ \underline{3} \\ \hline \end{array}$$

6 17 times 4

7 44 divided by 4

8 Share 35 by 5

9 47 × 2

10 Divide 74 by 2

11 27 ÷ 3

12 The product of 98 and 10

13 51 × 10

14 83 × 100

15 Share 76 between 4

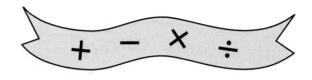

Copy these sums into your book.
You can use columns.
Work out the answers.

Exercise 39

1 $43 + 29$

2 The difference between 62 and 18

3 29×3

4 $75 \div 3$

5 Share 54 between 3

6 148 multiplied by 4

7 61 take away 27

8
$$\begin{array}{r} 8\ 8 \\ -\ 4\ 9 \\ \hline \end{array}$$

9
$$\begin{array}{r} 2\ 3\ 8 \\ \times \quad 5 \\ \hline \end{array}$$

10 $77 + 37$

11 108 subtract 11

12 Divide 232 by 2

13
$$\begin{array}{r} 5\ 6 \\ +\ 4\ 5 \\ \hline \end{array}$$

14 The sum of 23 and 65

Exercise 40

1 $19 + 79$

2 The difference between 93 and 27

3 17×5

4 $90 \div 10$

5 Share 69 between 3

6 98 multiplied by 2

7 51 take away 32

8
$$\begin{array}{r} 4\ 2 \\ -\ 3\ 3 \\ \hline \end{array}$$

9
$$\begin{array}{r} 1\ 8\ 6 \\ \times \quad 3 \\ \hline \end{array}$$

10 $68 + 68$

11 48 subtract 39

12 Divide 84 by 3

13
$$\begin{array}{r} 7\ 3 \\ +\ 1\ 7 \\ \hline \end{array}$$

14 The sum of 6 and 89

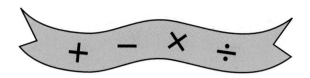

Copy these sums into your book.
You can use columns.
Work out the answers.

Exercise 41

1 $34 + 92$

2 The difference between 52 and 28

3 37×4

4 $55 \div 5$

5 Share 72 between 3

6 232 multiplied by 4

7 37 take away 19

8
```
   6 5
 − 5 1
 ─────
```

9
```
   1 4 1
 ×     5
 ───────
```

10 $85 + 32$

11 78 subtract 62

12 Divide 522 by 2

13
```
   7 7
 + 4 4
 ─────
```

14 The sum of 65 and 64

Exercise 42

1 $37 + 76$

2 The difference between 63 and 24

3 26×5

4 $70 \div 10$

5 Share 35 between 5

6 76 multiplied by 2

7 33 take away 17

8
```
   5 6
 − 3 8
 ─────
```

9
```
   2 7 1
 ×     3
 ───────
```

10 $46 + 82$

11 340 subtract 39

12 Divide 132 by 3

13
```
   6 1
 + 5 8
 ─────
```

14 The sum of 27 and 53

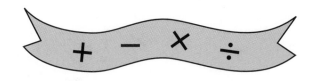

Copy these sums into your book.
You can use columns.
Work out the answers.

Exercise 43

1 56 + 51

2 The difference between 54 and 16

3 25 × 3

4 54 ÷ 2

5 Share 74 between 2

6 55 multiplied by 5

7 73 take away 37

8
```
   4 7
 - 3 8
 ─────
```

9
```
   4 5
 ×   5
 ─────
```

10 331 + 307

11 22 subtract 19

12 Divide 982 by 2

13
```
   3 4 7
 +   4 6
 ───────
```

14 The sum of 94 and 31

Exercise 44

1 82 + 12

2 The difference between 43 and 25

3 23 × 5

4 120 ÷ 10

5 Share 76 between 4

6 44 multiplied by 4

7 48 take away 39

8
```
   5 3
 - 4 2
 ─────
```

9
```
   4 9 1
 ×     2
 ───────
```

10 123 + 458

11 56 subtract 23

12 Divide 345 by 3

13
```
   2 4 1
 +   1 7
 ───────
```

14 The sum of 53 and 75